SIOUX
Indian Leaders

Sioux Indian village. Crazy Horse lived in a village such as this. (Photo from the Morrow collection, by courtesy of the University of South Dakota Museum)

SIOUX Indian Leaders

by

Mildred Fielder

BONANZA BOOKS · NEW YORK

This edition is published by Bonanza Books,
distributed by Crown Publishers, Inc.,
by arrangement with Superior Publishing Company.

h g f e d c b
BONANZA EDITION 1981

PRINTED IN THE UNITED STATES OF AMERICA

Library of Congress Cataloging in Publication Data

Fielder, Mildred.
    Sioux Indian leaders.

    Reprint. Originally published: Seattle:
Superior, 1975.
    Bibliography: p.
    Includes index.
    1. Dakota Indians—Biography.
2. Dakota Indians—History. I. Title.
E99.D1F5 1981   978'.00497   [B]   81-18158
ISBN 0-517-36954-0   AACR2

Dedication

To the many fine Sioux people of today
who are reaching toward the future
with confidence and pride in America.

CONTENTS

Page

Chapter One   Crazy Horse, The Warrior 11

Chapter Two   Spotted Tail, The Strategist .25

Chapter Three   Sitting Bull, Hunkpapa Medicine Man 40

Chapter Four   Gall, Reno's Opponent 57

Chapter Five   Martin Charger, and the Shetak Captives 72

Chapter Six   Red Cloud, the Schemer 90

Chapter Seven   Chauncey Yellow Robe, Bridge Between Two Cultures 112

Chapter Eight   Ben Reifel, Sioux Congressman 127

ILLUSTRATIONS

Page

American Horse 95
Appropriations committee meeting, 1964, Washington, D.C. 143
Bad Lands 53
Benteen, Captain F. W. 60
Big Foot dead at Wounded Knee 54
Black Hills race track, relief map 75
Buffalo 59
Buffalo and railroad train 42
Buffalo being killed by Indians 114
Buffalo Bill's Wild West show and Indians 49
Buffalo skinned on prairie 30
Buffalo skull 160
Charger, Martin 73
Charger, Samuel and Luke Gilbert 86
Chauncey Yellow Robe, see Yellow Robe, Chauncey
Cheyenne Indians skinning beef 31
Cheyenne warriors 44
Cheyenne warriors 85
Cody, Buffalo Bill 115
Coolidge ceremony, Deadwood 1927 121
Coolidge ceremony, Deadwood 1927 122
Coolidge, President Calvin, wearing Indian headdress 123
Crazy Horse, bust by Berke 21
Crook, General George 18
Crook's army near Buffalo Gap, 1870's 97
Custer Battlefield, bluffs where Reno fought 69
Custer Battlefield, Company I troopers at Keogh's grave, 1877 65
Custer Battlefield, horse bones on Custer's hill, 1877 64
Custer Battlefield, Indian lecturers 71
Custer Battlefield map 66
Custer Battlefield, Mass Monument 67
Custer Battlefield Museum 70
Custer Battlefield, Reno Monument 67
Custer Battlefield, Custer stone 71
Custer, General George and Osage scouts 19
Custer's Expedition to the Black Hills, 1874 56
Enlisted men in camp 62
Far West streamer taking cargo 68
Fetterman Monument 16
Fetterman Monument 92
Fool Soldiers Monument in City Park, Mobridge 87
Fool Soldiers Monument in Riverside Park 87
Fort Berthold Indian Agency office at Elbowoods 134

Fort Berthold Indian Reservation map, 1973 139
Fort Leavenworth, 1858 28
Fort Pierre, 1832 80
Four Bears 77
Four Bears Monument 88
Gall 58
Garrison Dam, photo 137
Garrison Dam, map 138
Garry Owen Historical marker 70
Harney, General William S....................... 21
Issuing rations, 1882 46
LaPlant, Louis 82
Little Big Horn River ford where Reno crossed 69
Little Wound 99
Mandan Chiefs................................. 76
Mandan Chiefs.................................136
Mandans, Hidatsa and Arikara group...............135
Martin Charger, see Charger, Martin
McGillycuddy, Dr. Valentine T. 99
Miles, General Nelson A.......................... 19
Military men in Dakota Territory 61
Oahe Irrigation meeting, Washington, D.C..........143
Officers of the western army 63
Pattee, Colonel John at his home.................. 83
Peace commissioners, Fort Laramie 94
Pine Ridge Agency, 1880's 101
Pine Ridge Agency, issue day 98
Pine Ridge Agency, white leaders and Indians 103
Powder River 17
Powder River 43
Rapid City, South Dakota, 1902 116
Red Cloud and his wife 93
Red Cloud, Graves photo 91
Red Cloud, Jack, son of Red Cloud 109
Red Cloud, Robinson photo 110
Red Cloud, South Dakota Historical Society photo 110
Red Cloud under arrest at Fort Robinson, 1882 107
Red Dog 96
Reifel, Ben 128
Reifel, Ben and Alice Johnson 132
Reifel, Ben and Barry Goldwater 142
Reifel, Ben and former President Eisenhower 142
Reifel, Ben and his family 141
Reifel, Ben and Loyce 145
Reifel, Ben and President Richard Nixon 145
Reifel, Ben and Scouters 140
Reifel, Ben, Extension Agent at Pine Ridge 133
Reifel, Ben, freshman in college 131
Reifel, Ben, honorary degree South Dakota State College ...147
Reifel, Ben, honorary degree University of South Dakota ...147
Reifel, Ben, with sod house 132
Reifel, Ben, R.O.T.C. uniform 131
Reifel, Ben, Jewel Cave Dedication 148

Reifel, Ben with South Dakota visitors in front of Capitol 144
Reifel, Mr. and Mrs. Ben Reifel and family 146
Reifel, Mr. and Mrs. campaigning 144
Reifel, Mr. and Mrs. William Reifel and sons 130
Reifel, William's farm 129
Reno, Major Marcus A. 60
Rescue of the Shetak Captives, mural 81
Rosebud Agency, 1885 38
Sheridan, General Philip 18
Sioux delegation to Washington 1875 85
Sioux grave, 1850 79
Sioux Indian village   2
Sioux Oglala delegation to Washington, 1880 105
Sioux squaws captured from Sitting Bull, 1877 45
Sitting Bull and Buffalo Bill Cody 50
Sitting Bull and his autograph 41
Sitting Bull, National Archives 41
Sitting Bull, Price collection 47
Sitting Bull's camp 45
Sitting Bull, squaw and twins 48
Spotted Tail and his sons at Carlisle 37
Spotted Tail, Bell photo 26
Spotted Tail, Kingsbury photo 29
Spotted Tail, Nebraska State Historical Society photo 109
Spotted Tail, Ulke painting 34
Spotted Tail's wife 29
Steamboat landing at Yankton, Dakota Territory, 1878 84
Sun Dance 32
Sword, Captain, Smithsonian photo 104
Sword, Captain, South Dakota Historical Society photo 20
Two Strike 33
Two Strike, Crow Dog and High Hawk 47
Two Strike's and Crow Dog's camp 33
United States Indian School, boy's dormitory 119
United States Indian School, main building 118
White scout scalps the savage 12
Woman's Dress 20
Wounded Knee, frozen bodies on ground 54
Yellow Robe, Chauncey, 1927 120
Yellow Robe, Chauncey and family 117
Yellow Robe, Chauncey as a young man 115
Yellow Robe, Chauncey, Vik photo 123
Yellow Robe, Chauncey, Vik photo 113
Young Man Afraid of His Horses, Cross photo 14
Young Man Afraid of His Horses, Smithsonian photo 102

ACKNOWLEDGEMENTS

A short article relating part of the information about Martin Charger was written by Mildred Fielder, titled "The Fool Soldiers," published by *True West*, June 1962.

The portion regarding Chauncey Yellow Robe speaking on experimental radio was originally published by the *Rapid City Journal*, May 11, 1969, Rapid City, South Dakota, under title "War Whoop!". That article was awarded a first place in the South Dakota State Fair for 1968, and a second place in South Dakota state contests by the South Dakota Press Women in 1969.

An article titled "South Dakota Sioux: First Bridge between Red and White," concerning Chauncey Yellow Robe, was published by the *Billings Gazette*, July 23, 1972, Billings, Montana.

I am indebted to the kindness of Ben Reifel for permission to research the story of his life, and to an unpublished autobiography written by Alice Reifel before her death which was made available to me for the Reifel story. Almost all quotes attributed to Mr. Reifel come from a personal interview with him, and all quotations from Alice originate in the manuscript which she wrote primarily as a family history for her grandchildren.

The prompt attention to my queries given by Shirley Luikens, Program Assistant in the Office of Indian Programs, National Park Service, was also greatly appreciated.

Most photos for the Reifel story are by courtesy of the Reifel family, except those few credited to other sources with the photo by-line. Photos and maps of Fort Berthold, Garrison Dam, and Indians of that area were furnished by Rev. H. W. Case.

In assembling the material on Chauncey Yellow Robe and his family I am indebted for the help from Marian Bedsaul, the Homestake Library, Lead, South Dakota; Helen Hoyt, the Rapid City Public Library, Rapid City, South Dakota; Paulette Hudson and Rena McGhan, the Sioux Indian Museum and Craft Center, Rapid City; and Katherine Thornby, Adams Memorial Museum, Deadwood, South Dakota.

Permission to quote has been received by:
Captain Louis M. McDermott, "The Primary Role of the Military on the Dakota Frontier," *South Dakota History*, Winter, 1971.
South Dakota Historical Society, Volumes V, XXII, and XXVIII.
Stanford University Press, *McGillycuddy: Agent,* by Julia B. McGillycuddy.

Mildred Fielder
2525 Bay Vista Lane
Los Osos, Calif. 93402

1

CRAZY HORSE, THE WARRIOR

Why Crazy Horse?

What business has he on that mountain top?

North of Custer in the Black Hills of South Dakota, not far from famed Mount Rushmore, sculptor Korczak Ziolkowski is carving a gigantic monument on Thunderhead Mountain which he calls "Crazy Horse." Though the project is not finished, the monument will depict an Indian warrior astride his horse with finger pointing forward, the largest monument in recorded history. It is estimated that four thousand men will be able to stand on Crazy Horse's outstretched arm alone when the monument is complete.

But why Crazy Horse, when the Sioux had so many outstanding leaders during its years of rebellion against white encroachment of the western lands?

He was a young man with a gut hatred for the whites. He was a fighting fool during the whole of his short life. He was a war strategist who led the Indians to victories they had never imagined possible. He was martyred in a betrayal by his own people, and killed by them in unexpected drama.

Is that enough?

Let's look at his record.

Nine Sioux tribes lived west of the Missouri River in the last half of the nineteenth century, more than half of whom were either Oglalas or Brule Indians. Crazy Horse was an Oglala, son of a holy man named Crazy Horse and a Brule woman who was sister to the noted chief Spotted Tail. The official encyclopedic report of his life says he was born in 1849. Mari Sandoz, who researched his life thoroughly through interviews with Indians who had known Crazy Horse, says he was born around 1842. Since Crazy Horse died a young man, this difference in years makes him either 28 when he was killed, or 35.

Mari Sandoz' account must be considered authentic, she gives detailed bibliography and notes for her sources. Though she says flatly that Crazy Horse was a Lakota Sioux, an Oglala born of a Brule mother and an Oglala father in an Oglala Indian village, she hints broadly again and again that he may have been the son of an unnamed, unknown white man. It is possible. In the 1840's it was not unusual for an Indian maiden to be known by a white trader or soldier in a brief encounter.

As a boy he was known as Curly because he had yellow hair with a tendency to curl and brown eyes, contrasting the darker skin and straight black hair of the Sioux Indians. Later his hair darkened to light brown but it was never the black of the Sioux and his skin was always paler than his brothers. He looked so much like a white man's child that emigrants repeatedly asked if he were a captive white boy.

Crazy Horse resented the implication fiercely. He knew he was Indian. The entire tribe knew he was Indian. Yet there it was—he looked like a white boy. The differences were subtle and inner.

He was a savage in all the ways he knew of living. His love and loyalty lay with the Sioux people of whom he was a part, but his instincts were different than theirs. A quiet boy of few words, he had no heart for the Sun Dance, the taking of scalps, the counting of coups in battle—yet he was braver than any of his Indian brothers when fighting the white soldiers. His biographers credit his bravery with a vision he had as a boy which promised him that no bullets nor arrows from enemies could kill him, only his own people could harm him. His vision seemed true.

No wonder the Oglalas called him Strange Man.

He was taught the basic lessons of warfare by a friend, Hump the Oglala warrior, and he was guided by an Oglala medicine man named Chips, a man whose

"knowledge of the supernatural was uncanny." [1]

The boy, Curly, being the son of a holy man was thus not a hereditary chief and had to earn the title by his own efforts. Crazy Horse the Holy Man had tried to change the name of Curly to His Horse Looking after the boy killed his first buffalo and caught a wild horse by himself, but the name Curly remained until he fought against neighboring Indian tribes around 1859 with considerable honor to himself. Crazy Horse the Holy Man thereupon gave Curly his own name, and

A white scout scalps the savage as a token of victory. Crazy Horse was incensed at the whites for their treatment of the Indian, though the Sioux were as merciless in their warfare. (Photo from the Morrow collection, by courtesy of the University of South Dakota Museum)

took the name of Worm for himself. If Crazy Horse was born in 1849 that would make him rather young to be fighting as a warrior, but dates of Indian births are not definite and one can just as well accept the earlier date of 1842, a more plausible one.

Part of the Crazy Horse story is the love he had as a young man for a niece of Red Cloud, Black Buffalo Woman, and must be mentioned because of the after effects of that love. Quiet as he was, Crazy Horse was slow to mention his love in words. According to the Indian ways of life Black Buffalo Woman was given in marriage to No Water while Crazy Horse was on the warpath with some of his friends. He was completely despondent, but the deed was done. After a while Crazy Horse began to visit the camp of No Water from time to time and was able to see and talk to Black Buffalo Woman. It was in that camp, too, that he became acquainted with Chips, the medicine man.

Crazy Horse was adding to his reputation as a fighter, but he remained true to his vision and brought back no scalps, no coups, no horses for himself. He acted often in the scouting parties. He was one of the twenty decoys at the battle of Platte Bridge, July 25 and 26, 1865, who tried to coax white soldiers from the security of their forts so the waiting warriors could shoot them. The Sioux braves became too eager and could not wait, so the ruse failed.

Because of the failure of the Indian attacks the Sioux decided to re-organize. They chose a council of seven older advisors called the Big Bellies, with four young men, the Shirt Wearers, as leaders. Crazy Horse was named a Shirt Wearer. In doing so, Woman's Dress, son and grandson of a chief, was ignored for the honor, thus gaining his enmity for the rest of Crazy Horse's life. Both No Water and Woman's Dress were also members of the Bad Faces led by Red Cloud. The other three young men chosen as Shirt Wearers that day were Young Man Afraid of His Horses, Sword, and American Horse, all of them sons of hereditary chiefs.

In 1866 a treaty was signed by the Brules giving the whites a road and forts through the Powder River country, the good hunting lands of the Sioux. The Bozeman Trail was staked from Cheyenne to Bozeman, Montana, and still the Sioux did not realize what was happening. When they began to see emigrants crossing their Powder River hunting country, they knew and they took steps to stop it. The Bozeman Trail was so harassed by Sioux raiding parties that none dared travel it unless heavily protected by military guard.

December 21, 1866, the Sioux attacked Fort Phil Kearny, and in connection with that battle we find one of the earliest white historical records mentioning Crazy Horse.

Captain William Judd Fetterman was stationed at Fort Phil Kearny at the time. About two thousand warriors were hovering nearby. A small number of their best riders, including Crazy Horse, were sent from the hidden main body to coax the soldiers from the fort by stampeding some government horses. Soldiers under Captain Fetterman emerged from the fort to recover the stock. Fetterman followed the decoys to the hidden Sioux, where the triumphant warriors erupted in full force and killed ninety soldiers.

Six months later, July 31, 1867, a second attack near the fort resulted in the Wagon Box Fight in which the tables were turned and thirty two soldiers defended themselves against a large body of Indians. Crazy Horse and Hump were in that battle, but the Sioux were fighting in the traditional way of every man for himself.

According to Indian friends, Crazy Horse and his friend He Dog were made lance bearers and thus leaders of a war party against the Crows with lodges and women accompanying it. Crazy Horse had continued to see Black Buffalo Woman, and at that time she placed her three children with relatives and joined Crazy Horse on the hunt. Lakota women were free to come and go as they please, but Black Buffalo Woman was married to an important man in the Bad Faces group, and No Water did not take kindly to the idea of losing his woman. While they were still on the expedition No Water tracked them down and shot Crazy Horse through the upper jaw under the nose. For a time they wondered if he would live, but he did. Black Buffalo Woman was returned to her lodge. As a reprimand the Big Bellies of Crazy Horse's village demanded that he return the shirt of the Shirt Wearers. He did so, but his reputation among those who knew him remained untarnished. He was a leader. They would follow him.

Nevertheless members of his tribe decided he needed a wife and made arrangements for Black Shawl, a young Oglala girl, to marry him. He learned to cherish Black Shawl, and for the sake of peace among the Oglalas he gave up seeing Black Buffalo Woman completely, even when he heard the next spring that she had given birth to a pale skinned, light haired daughter like himself.

Black Shawl also gave him a daughter, a babe whom they named They Are Afraid of Her. Crazy Horse loved her dearly. When he was gone on a war expedition one year, she died. He blamed her death on the whites, as the disease that took her was a white man's disease.

The Indian hostilities lessened somewhat in the Powder River area for a while, but Red Cloud and his hostiles continued to harass white intruders along the entire Bozeman Trail until in 1868 the United States government withdrew its forces from the Powder River country and the Sioux burned the abandoned Fort Phil Kearny to the ground.

Young Man Afraid of His Horses (name sometimes shortened to Young Man Afraid) was one of the hereditary chiefs selected by the Oglalas as a Shirt Wearer at the same time the honor was given to Crazy Horse. (Photo by W. R. Cross, from the collection of Carl Leedy)

In 1868 one of the most important treaties with the Sioux Indians was conducted at Fort Laramie. It was signed by 184 Sioux chiefs from eleven tribes. The treaty designated all of the present South Dakota land west of the Missouri River as a Sioux reservation. It suggested that the Indians abandon their nomadic life in favor of peaceful living in that reservation, and in return the United States government promised individual tracts of land to each Indian, education for their children, grants of clothing, money and cattle. The Indians agreed not to oppose railroad construction, not to attack people traveling across the prairies, to cease war in general, while the United States promised to abandon military posts within the territory.

Such well known Indian chiefs as Spotted Tail, Sitting Bull the Oglala, Red Cloud, Young Man Afraid of His Horses were signed on that treaty, but the name of Crazy Horse was not. This has been explained by the statement that Sitting Bull (Hunkpapa) and Crazy Horse led two non-agency bands of Indians, and Crazy Horse

> "never came into an agency until his surrender in 1877, but his uncle, Little Hawk, had led a portion of his followers to Fort Laramie in 1868 to sign the treaty and get a share of the guns and ammunition being given out." [2]

In the years following the signing of the Laramie treaty of 1868 the United States government tried to institute a peace policy among the Sioux, trying to teach the Indian that with his buffalo gone from the prairies and the inevitable white movement into the west that he must learn to live with the new civilization.

The new policy might have worked except for Indian resentment of four things. They did not like telegraph wires crossing their lands. They feared the Northern Pacific Railroad that crossed the land from the Missouri River to the Yellowstone, insisting that the railroad drove what little game was left from the area. They complained that Indian agents were not giving them their just rations but withholding some for themselves. And fourth, they bitterly resisted the growing interest in the Black Hills.

The hatred of Crazy Horse for the whites was growing more intense year by year. He watched while General George A. Custer led an expedition into the Black Hills in 1874, a portion definitely included in the great Sioux lands by the last treaty. He knew that Walter Jenney led a second expedition into the Black Hills the next summer. Desperately, Crazy Horse led his warriors against the white invaders in skirmishes meant to discourage them from further entering .

In an effort to control general Indian depredations in the west, the Government issued an order December 3, 1875 directing all Sioux to be within their reservations before January 31, 1876, or to be considered hostiles. It was winter, a difficult time for traveling, and many of the Indians did not comply. On February 7, 1876, Lt. General P. H. Sheridan was given authority to control the absent Indians.

The plan of the campaign sent military expeditions into Powder River and Yellowstone River country under three generals, Brigadier General George Crook, General John Gibbon, and General Terry. March 17, 1876 the Oglalas were attacked on the west side of Powder River by a division of Crook's army led by Colonel Reynolds. Surprised and defeated, the Indians saw the soldiers burn their village and drive off their horses. Led by He Dog, they joined the Crazy Horse village at some distance, determined to strike against the whites at the earliest opportunity.

It was time for a war council. Word went with Indian runners to the Sioux tribes. Crazy Horse would lead them against the whites. By that time the Sioux believed completely in the great powers of the Oglala Strange Man. He would be their new chief. From all parts of the western prairies the Sioux began gathering on the Powder River, bringing their women, their lodges with them.

Crazy Horse planned his battle tactics well. He delegated the older men to stay with the lodges as guards. He emphasized that the old way of making war was no longer good. The warriors must act as one body under one leadership. There must be no coups counted, no scalps, no victory dances. Only by a concentration on killing could they hope to regain their lands.

On June 17, 1876, Crazy Horse and his fighters met General Crook at the Battle of the Rosebud. It was a hard fought battle on both sides. The Lakotas began to retreat, but Crazy Horse rallied them with cries of encouragement and they turned to follow him again into battle. The soldiers swung around and struck the rear guard of the Indians, but were breaking under the pressure of the fight. Sioux shells were gone and the Indians scattered, but Crook had been stopped in his tracks.

The Fetterman Monument, Wyoming, 1971, marking the site of the Fetterman Massacre of December 21, 1868. Crazy Horse was one of the decoys at the battle in which eighty or ninety soldiers were killed. Historical sources differ on the number. (Photo by Fielder)

The Powder River, Wyoming, at Interstate 90 from the west bank, 1971. Crazy Horse and his village lived near the Powder River at times. The great encampment of Sioux prior to the Battle of the Little Big Horn was also along the Powder River. (Photo by Fielder)

Crazy Horse's magic had been with him through the battle. Later Big Bat Pourier, a trader's son, said to a reporter,

> "You can call it medicine or anything you want to, but I saw Crazy Horse at the Rosebud Creek charge straight into Crook's army, and it seemed every soldier and Indian we had with us took a shot at him and they couldn't even hit his horse." [3]

The battle finished, Crazy Horse realized that the Indian warriors had fought as he had instructed, together rather than individually for their own glory. For the first time they had defeated the whites in a major confrontation.

The gathering of Sioux tribes had increased to some 12,000 to 15,000 Indians, their lodges, women, children, old men and warriors. The northern Cheyenne were led by Chiefs Two Moon and White Bull. Crazy Horse, Low Dog and Big Road headed the Oglalas. The Hunkpapas had come from the northern plains led by medicine man Sitting Bull and Chiefs Gall, Crow King and Black Moon. Hump brought the Minneconjous, and Spotted Eagle his Sans-Arc people. Rain in the Face was reported to be another chief in the group.

Six days later on June 24, 1876 the great gathering of Sioux lodges was moved across the Little Big Horn in an orderly procession directed by a designated herald. By the end of the day the Sioux encampment consisted of five big circles with two or three smaller groups, the whole extending three miles up and down the river. They were a joyous gathering. That night the Sioux danced for the sheer fun of being together. The young women and the young warriors looked at each other and sang with no thought of war in their minds.

It was the day before the Battle of the Little Big Horn.

Of the great mass of warriors, Sitting Bull was the acknowledged leader of the northern Indians, the Hunkpapas, and Crazy Horse controlled the rest. Sitting Bull was not a fighting chief, but his influence was so strong among his followers

17

that he was the planner, the commander whom his warriors trusted implicitly. Greatest of the Hunkpapa warrior chiefs was Gall.

Most historians give credit to Sitting Bull as the master mind behind the overall strategy of that day, but say that Crazy Horse attacked Custer and Gall attacked Reno. Sitting Bull's and Gall's later reports of the battles verify this. Mari Sandoz states that Crazy Horse counciled with Sitting Bull before the hostilities began.

General Terry had divided his command in two, a column under Gibbon marching up the Yellowstone River toward the Tongue River, Custer leading the Seventh Cavalry up Rosebud Creek to follow a broad Indian trail. The two forces meant to catch the Indians between them.

Custer found the smoke of the Sioux gathering and rode toward it with all speed. Around noon of June 25 he divided his command into three parts, one headed by Major Marcus A. Reno, another under Captain Frederick W. Benteen, the third by himself, the object again being to catch the Indians in a trap. Benteen crossed to the left of the trail. Custer and Reno followed on opposite banks of a creek toward the Little Big Horn Valley and the Indian encampment.

When they saw portions of the Indian lodges ahead of them Reno was directed to charge the camp. Custer turned right to attack the village from the rear. Reno rode into the village but it seemed deserted. Many years later Sitting Bull told newspaper men that he, Sitting Bull, had ordered evacuation of the villages when Indian Scouts caught sight of the blue coats moving their way in order to save the women, children, and old men from annihilation.

Reno and his men were immediately surrounded by Indian warriors. In the battle which followed, Reno first ordered his men to dismount and fight on foot but they were forced into a timber thicket. For a short time the soldiers held that point, then Reno ordered them to remount and retreat to the bluffs overlooking the valley. On the bluffs they dug in and poured lead into the battling Indians.

While Reno was fighting Gall, Custer and his men were discovered by Crazy Horse, his Oglalas and the Cheyennes, and the battle began. When Reno gained

General Philip Sheridan was given the responsibility of bringing the hostile Indian bands into the Indian reservations on February 7, 1876, the order which ultimately resulted in the massacre of Custer and the Seventh Cavalry at the Battle of the Little Big Horn. (Photo by courtesy of National Archives)

General George Crook, who fought Crazy Horse's warriors at Rosebud Creek June 17, 1876, and admitted that Crazy Horse won the battle. (Photo by courtesy of Smithsonian Institution National Anthropological Archives)

the prominence of the bluffs and a superior fighting position over Gall's forces, Gall turned his fighters to help Crazy Horse against Custer. The overwhelming force of several thousand crazy-mad Sioux were thus entirely concentrated momentarily on Custer and his men. Custer's entire force was killed.

Reno recuperated on the bluffs. As he waited, Captain Benteen's troopers joined him. It seemed best to maintain their position. The night gave them some rest, but when dawn came on the 26th the Indians were still pouring bullets and arrows into the white forces.

Toward the middle of the afternoon the Indians began to withdraw. Sitting Bull said later that they quit because there had been enough killing and they wanted no more. Others said the withdrawal of the Indians was because of the approach of Terry's other flank which could be seen coming across the prairie. Remembering that the Sioux had all of their people with them, it is altogether possible that both statements had a ring of truth in them. They saw Terry coming, and they wanted no more battle when the odds became increasingly against them.

The Sioux set fire to the grass in the valley and the entire Indian nation moved up the river toward the Big Horn Mountains.

It had seemed to be an astonishing victory for the Sioux, but Crazy Horse sensed that it was not so. The story of the day was immediately a legend in the campfires, but there was something else too, a huddling together, a fear of retaliation

General George A. Custer and his Indian scouts, picture dated 1867. Crazy Horse was believed to be the first Indian leader to attack Custer at the Battle of the Little Big Horn. (Photo from Elizabeth Custer, *Following the Guidon*, 1890)

General Nelson A. Miles, who attacked Crazy Horse's village January 8, 1877. (Photo from the National Archives)

Sword, of the Pine Ridge Indian police, was one of the leaders of delegations sent to Crazy Horse in 1877 to persuade him to surrender. (Photo from South Dakota Historical Society)

Woman's Dress, one of the betrayers of Crazy Horse at Red Cloud Agency in 1877. (Photo from *Rapid City Daily Journal*)

by the whites. Sitting Bull and his followers, chased by General Miles, fled to Canada where they were safe. Crazy Horse led his people north where they were safely entrenched for the winter. He himself with a few of his trusted friends such as He Dog, Short Bull, Black Fox, turned toward the Black Hills to raid the white wagon trains or make sneak attacks on the miners who were filtering into the Black Hills.

General Sibley's scouts caught a band of Sioux on July 7 of that year, killing many of them. Colonel Merritt attacked Cheyennes ten days later on July 17, and Crazy Horse's good friend Yellow Hand was killed. Crazy Horse knew of these things, indeed may have been at the scene of the battle.

He was said by some historians to be at the battle of Slim Buttes north of the Black Hills on September 9, 1876, but a report of the battle submitted to the war department stated:

> "I learn from the prisoners that Crazy Horse, with the Cheyennes, a village of some three hundred lodges, was within eight or ten miles, and that the strength of the village taken consisted of about two hundred souls, 100 of them warriors." [4]

The treaty ceding the Black Hills to the United States Government was being prepared. October 27, 1876, it was ready, and the Indians at the agencies were called for their signatures. According to Mari Sandoz' interviews with the Indians, the Sioux were locked in the stockade and told that they must sign the treaty or their children would not be fed. After two days, they signed.

According to white historians, there was no choice. To protect the white miners and their families, to shield the moving wave of white emigration toward the west, the United States Government was in no position to bargain further with the red men. The massacre of Custer's Seventh Cavalry was a bitter memory. With Sioux numbering 4,901 Indians at Red Cloud Agency, signatures on that Black Hills Treaty included such noted names as the Oglala chiefs Young Man Afraid of His Horses, Red Cloud and Big Foot, and Spotted Tail of the Brules.

Crazy Horse was one of the two leaders of the roving hostiles, the other being Sitting Bull who was safe in Canada. Crazy Horse was thus instinctively named as the leader of any terrorizing for the rest of the year. He had not joined the agency Indians in the treaty of the Black Hills, and he did not intend to join them afterwards. Nevertheless, things were going against him.

His people were hungry. Crazy Horse stole cattle from General Miles' military camp on the Tongue River to feed his people. When Chief Dull Knife and his son were both killed by white soldiers on November 25, even the Oglalas became uneasy. Some of the Oglalas tried to sneak away from Crazy Horse's camp at night to go to the supposed safety of the agencies, but he found them and stopped them, angry at their abandonment of his leadership.

From the Red Cloud Agency, General Crook sent several delegations to the Tongue River country to persuade Crazy Horse that he must surrender. Crook promised that if Crazy Horse would come he could have an agency of his own at a place chosen by himself.

At the same time, two messengers from the northern agencies in Dakota Territory approached Crazy Horse. He would not listen to them. The winter was cold, his provisions low, and the spirit of the Oglalas was broken so completely that when General Miles attacked the village of Crazy Horse January 8, 1877, the Oglalas did little else than retreat while the warriors guarded their rear.

Sword with thirty Sioux, including Woman's Dress, was the first delegation to reach Crazy Horse from the Red Cloud Agency. Crazy Horse would not talk to him but went into the hills alone to think.

General Miles and Crook sent Big Leggins, a trader's son, with more offers to Crazy Horse. Then Spotted Tail himself led a delegation to talk to the Oglalas with the promise of rations, clothing, and freedom to return to the north when spring came. Spotted Tail did not tell them that if they went to the agency they would lose their horses and arms.

Crazy Horse finally faced the most difficult decision in his life. His people were cold, hungry, desperate and attacked on all sides. After a day alone on the hillsides Crazy Horse came back to accept Spotted Tail's inducements. They

Bust of Crazy Horse by Ernest Berke, New York, 1957, for which Berke is said to have used a photograph called "Crazy Horse." It is generally conceded that Crazy Horse, the warrior, was never photographed, and the photograph in question is that of the second husband of Nellie Larrabee who took the name of Crazy Horse as a mark of honor in the warrior's memory. (Photo by courtesy of Joe Koller)

General William S. Harney (Photo from the collection of S. Goodale Price)

picked up their tepees, their lodges, their travois, and began the long trail to the Red Cloud Agency.

May 6, 1877, Crazy Horse led his Oglalas into the agency, but it was not a surrender. Riding straight and proud on his pony, he was followed by nearly a thousand people singing as they came.

He did not object when the soldiers took their horses, their guns, their ammunition. He had come in peace. He intended to stay in peace for the good of his people, and he would cooperate.

They gave Crazy Horse and the Oglalas a place to pitch their tepees about three miles from the agency buildings, close enough for constant surveillance, far enough that they could still be one group. Once there, he tried to talk to the generals about his promised agency but nobody would discuss it with him. Black Shawl was increasingly sick. He called the white doctor to treat her. He tried his best to know what was wanted of the Oglalas, talking to the soldiers when they asked about the Indian battles, asking for rations, clothing, whatever was needed for his starving people. Gradually the military men gave him a grudging respect. They saw him for what he was, a quiet modest man of superior intelligence, a man concerned for the welfare of his people rather than for his own glory.

The Indians already established at the agency could see the friendliness developing between Crazy Horse and the generals, and resented it. Woman's Dress was there, he who had been bypassed as a Shirt Wearer so many years ago in favor of the boy Curly. Red Cloud was there, he who had been ignored by the Oglalas as a chief when the much younger Crazy Horse had been elevated to high rank in the tribe. No Water was there, he whose wife Black Buffalo Woman had loved Crazy Horse enough to leave her husband. Between them, they began to influence the young friendlies around the fort against Crazy Horse.

Sensing his restlessness, the generals asked Crazy Horse to be a scout for them on the northern plains. At first he would not, but then accepted because at least he could be a hunter again rather than doing nothing on the agency grounds.

In the background, the insidious whispers circulated—Crazy Horse was a dangerous man, Crazy Horse would turn on the whites when he got the chance. Inevitably, as they were meant to do, the whispers reached the white generals.

Crazy Horse was a lonely leader during those summer months. Black Shawl was getting somewhat better but was still a sick woman. Perhaps because of his loneliness, perhaps urged by his friends and the military officers themselves, he took as a second wife Nellie, the pretty daughter of Joe Larrabee, trader at the agency.

When a feast was suggested for the Crazy Horse lodges, the jealous ones under Red Cloud insisted on talking to the agent and told him that Crazy Horse was a wild warrior not to be trusted. A proposed buffalo hunt was cancelled, but still Crazy Horse was held in high esteem on the reservation. When Congress proposed to send the Oglalas and the Brules to the Missouri River with Crazy Horse as head chief, a council was held on the reservation under the leadership of General Clark.

Clark suggested that Crazy Horse go as scout to the Yellowstone region first,, but Crazy Horse said no, he was done fighting. They insisted. Finally Crazy Horse said, because he was trying to keep peace with the whites,

> "Myself and my people are tired of war. We have come in and surrendered to the Great Father and asked for peace. But now, if he wishes us to go to war again and asks our help, we will go north and fight till there is not a Nez Perces left." [5]

Clark's interpreter was Frank Grouard, a half-breed known as the Grabber by the Oglala and despised by them as a traitor to their race. Grouard interpreted

Crazy Horse's speech correctly until the last few words, and translated instead, "We will go north and fight till there is not a white man left." [6]

The words were a bombshell in the quiet of the council. Clark shouted angrily, quarreling erupted between Grouard and Louis Bordeaux, the second interpreter. In the general chaos, Crazy Horse and his followers left the room.

The report of Crazy Horse's supposed challenge raced over the telegraph wires. Though Grouard was forced to change his interpretation, nobody believed the second interpretation. A few days later Big Bat Pourier and Billy Garnett, interpreters, met Woman's Dress, who told them that Crazy Horse and his followers would be at the next council:

> "Crazy Horse is going to shake hands with General Clark then he is going to hold on to his hand, and his warriors are going to kill General Crook and his whole party." [7]

When pressed for further information, Woman's Dress said that Little Wolf had heard the plan when eavesdropping outside Crazy Horse's lodge and told Lone Bear, who told Woman's Dress.

Big Bat and Billy took the information to Clark, who believed it implicitly. He offered a reward of one hundred dollars for the killing of Crazy Horse, and No Water offered to accept the challenge. Somehow word reached Crazy Horse of the enmity against him. Leaving in the night, he took Black Shawl and a company of Oglalas and fled to the Spotted Tail Agency for the safekeeping of Black Shawl. There he was found by Clark and fifty five armed Indian scouts. When they demanded that he return to Fort Robinson, Crazy Horse agreed to do so if Black Shawl were left in safety.

When they reached Fort Robinson Crazy Horse was conducted directly to the guardhouse. As they approached the building he realized that it was a prison, a jail with iron bars. His lifelong horror of imprisonment washed over him, and as the door was being shut behind him he grabbed a hidden knife from his garments and lunged through the door in an attempt to gain his freedom.

Captain Kennington grabbed Crazy Horse's left arm, and his Oglala friend, Little Big Man, his right arm. Crazy Horse tried to wrench free, but could not. Red Cloud, American Horse, and other Sioux stood there watching, shouting to shoot him.

Dr. McGillycuddy remembered that one of the white soldiers thrust a bayonet into Crazy Horse's abdomen. Mari Sandoz says that Swift Bear and other Brules were helping Little Big Man hold him while the guard lunged the bayonet at Crazy Horse. Suddenly the Indians loosed their hold, but the deed was done. Crazy Horse had been mortally wounded.

They took him to the adjutant's office. His mother's uncle, Touch the Clouds, came and remained with him as he lay dying. His father, Worm, joined them after a while. There was nothing they could do. During the night of September 7, 1877, he died, betrayed and martyred by those he loved best, his own Sioux people.

His body was given to his band of Oglala Sioux for burial. They prepared the scaffold in a secret place said to be known only to his family and the medicine man Chips. Many years later a three quarter blood Sioux said that Crazy Horse was buried near Corn Creek Community, a small village long disappeared, once south of the White River in the Pine Ridge Reservation. In any event, nobody can say today the exact spot where Crazy Horse lies buried.

What did he accomplish?

He was called "premier warrior among the best warriors in the world," [8] "a greater cavalry leader than Custer, Sheridan, or Stuart," [9] "brilliant young warrior," [10] "the greatest of the Sioux warriors." [11] A reputation as a warrior alone is not enough, but Crazy Horse also taught by his example that it was better to fight for the common good than for one's individual glory.

He gave the Sioux hope when there was no hope, and he left a legend behind him that is remembered to this day. It is said that:

"Those who are lucky enough to be related to him are quite vain about it, and those who aren't, say Crazy Horse was a great hero." [12]

There was a mysticism about the man, an unexplained charisma that does not let the memory of him die. The Strange Man, his Oglala people called him. The Strange Man he remains.

In 1957 a bust of Crazy Horse was created by Ernest Berke of New York in which he used a picture alleged to be that of Crazy Horse as a model. Mari Sandoz supports the Sioux claim that there is no picture of Crazy Horse the warrior. She says the picture titled Crazy Horse is of a small dark Indian who was the second husband of Nellie Larrabee, a man who took the name of his predecesor as a mark of honor.

Korczak Ziolkowski has been a noted sculptor for most of his working life, and says the idea of a monument to the Sioux race was proposed to him by Chief Henry Standing Bear of Pine Ridge Agency, with the suggestion that Crazy Horse be the man portrayed. Ziolkowski came to South Dakota in 1940, chose Thunderhead Mountain for the work and tried to get federal help on the project. Being refused, he acquired the rights to the mountain and in 1948 began working alone.

Tourist revenue keeps the project going. Year by year Ziolkowski chisels more of the mountain to fit his proposed model, and gradually the form of the gigantic Crazy Horse is taking shape.

Some day, if all goes well, Crazy Horse may ride again.

References: Crazy Horse, the Warrior

[1] Herman, Eddie, "Noted Oglala Medicine Man Kept Crazy Horse's Secret," *Rapid City Journal,* February 11, 1951. Rapid City, South Dakota.

[2] Anderson, Harry H., "A History of the Cheyenne River Indian Agency and Its Military Post, Fort Bennett, 1868-1891," *South Dakota Historical Collections,* Volume XXVIII. Pierre, South Dakota, 1956, p.434.

[3] Herman, Eddie, opus cited.

[4] Kingsbury, George W., *History of Dakota Territory,* ed. by George Martin Smith. The S. J. Clarke Publishing Company, Chicago, 1915, Volume I, p. 958.

[5] McGillycuddy, Julia B., *McGillycuddy: Agent.* Stanford University Press, Stanford, Calif. 1941. p. 80.

[6] McGillicuddy, Julia B., opus cited, p. 80.

[7] Herman, Eddie, "Betrayer of Crazy Horse Disgraced," *Rapid City Daily Journal,* December 10, 1950. Rapid City, South Dakota.

[8] McDermott, Louis M., "The Primary Role of the Military on the Dakota Frontier," *South Dakota History,* Winter, 1971. p. 11.

[9] "Chicago Writer Discusses Last Stand of Custer," *Rapid City Daily Journal,* July 6, 1936. Rapid City, South Dakota.

[10] McGillycuddy, Julia B., opus cited, p. 47.

[11] McGillicuddy, Julia B., opus cited, p. 86.

[12] Lewis, Emily H., "Sioux Indians Believed in Seeing America First," *Rapid City Daily Journal,* August 30, 1959. Rapid City, South Dakota.

2

SPOTTED TAIL THE STRATEGIST

The soldiers came upon the Brule Indian camp unexpectedly, and when General William S. Harney gave the word, "Charge!" they charged with blood in their eyes. The Indian women and children were in their way, and they shot them as quickly as they killed the Indian braves. It was not much of a contest, being so unexpected to the Brule Sioux in that year of 1855. Yet they should have expected something of the kind.

Spotted Tail (Sinte Galeska) was thirty one years old, a warrior in the prime of his fighting ability. Some of the white dragoons were killed, but not enough. The Sioux survivors scattered, running for their lives, bayoneted when bullets were not quick enough and left to die along the trail.

Spotted Tail was sick at the sight. When the battle was over and the dragoons had spurred their horses from the campground, Spotted Tail's wife and one child were gone too, taken as hostages by the white soldiers.

It had not been an unprovoked attack. Harney, known as the Hornet by the Sioux Brules, had retaliated against Sioux attacks on the whites, and in the eyes of both sides it was one whip against another—yet Spotted Tail mourned for his people's misery.

The episode of the Mormon cow had started the open battles between the two, the Brules and the white soldiers. A weak old cow had wandered into the camp of Spotted Tail's band a year earlier. It had started as something funny for the Brules. When the cow stumbled around the campside a visiting Miniconjou named High Forehead had shot the ox with an arrow. The old cow was poor eating, but what was it doing in an Indian camp anyway?

The Mormon owner had demanded justice, he wanted his cow back. Brave Bear, head chief of the Brules of the Platte River had gone to the whites and tried to explain, even offering some of his finest horses in exchange for the old cow, but nothing would prevail. The Mormon wanted his cow back. Lieutenant Grattan was sent by the Commandant at Fort Laramie with a party of twenty three soldiers to the Indian camp to arrest High Forehead for the crime.

Brave Bear refused to give his guest to white arrest. In high impatience, Lieutenant Grattan ordered his men to shoot. In the fracas which followed Brave Bear was killed, but all of the white soldiers were killed, too. Maddened by the whole affair, the Brules raced toward the warehouse in which their annuity goods were stored and plundered the warehouse.

Brave Bear's death naturally had to be avenged. Red Leaf and Long Chin, Brave Bear's brothers, and his cousin Spotted Tail joined to lead the expedition. After the June Sun Dance, the Sioux went on the warpath. They intended primarily to attack their ancient traditional enemies, the Pawnees and Omahas, but fully expected to make their presence known to any white military men or emigrants as well.

It was then in some kind of retaliation that General Harney attacked the camp on the Bluewater Creek in 1855. Something had to be done to control the Brule fighters, and the only thing they knew was force.

To make his victory complete Harney demanded that the chief warriors of the Brules be given as prisoners to remind them not to attack the whites again. With great diffidence Spotted Tail and the other warriors leading the Bluewater fight accepted the sacrifice, and surrendered. The Brule fighters were conducted to Fort Leavenworth where they were held in captivity for a year.

For Spotted Tail, young Brule warrior, it was the most important year in his life. Until that time he had imagined the whites to be a few soldiers in the west who were a nuisance to the prairie Sioux. In Fort Leavenworth he saw the might of the white people, their military men in great force, their inexhaustible numbers.

He was not stupid. Spotted Tail was one of the most intelligent men ever known in the Brule camps. He saw. He learned while in Fort Leavenworth, and what he learned guided him the rest of his life. He realized that the Sioux could not keep the whites from the western plains by shooting them, by killing them. The only way the Sioux could survive in the future was by negotiation, by learning to read and write the English language, by thinking faster than the white soldiers or the white agents. There, in Fort Leavenworth, he decided to do this.

Spotted Tail had been born in 1823 (or 1824) on White River west of the Missouri River in southern South Dakota. His father was a Saone of the Blackfoot-Sioux named Cunka (Tangle Hair). His mother was a Brule named Walks With The Pipe. The name Spotted Tail became his when he was given a striped racoon tail by a white beaver trapper, and his boyhood name of Jumping Buffalo was discarded.

Spotted Tail's story is mixed with that of Crazy Horse, whose mother was Spotted Tail's sister; with that of Red Cloud, whose rise as a Sioux chief was at the same time as Spotted Tail's achievements; with that of his lifelong friend, Two Strike; and other eminent names of the Sioux of those years such as Young Man Afraid of His Horses, and Crow Dog.

Spotted Tail, Sioux chief.
Sioux spelling Sinte-Galeska or Sin-tig-a-les-ka. 1823-1881. (Bell photo, by courtesy of Adams Memorial Museum)

He was a scout by 1839, a boy in his 'teens, and it is estimated that he earned the rank of shirt wearer probably around ten years later when he was in his twenties. At the time of the Bluewater Creek fight, Spotted Tail was a shirt wearer, a warrior, but not yet a chief.

Spotted Tail and the others were treated with kindness at Leavenworth and released in the spring of 1856 under military escort. They remained at Fort Kearney on the Lower Platte from May to September 1856, when they went home to find Little Thunder head chief of the Brules.

From that time Spotted Tail began to get as much education as he could. He learned to read and write English, and he watched the ways of the whites at every opportunity. His keen mind noted the tricks played by Indian agents and traders, and he filed them for future use. For a few years the Brules lay low except for their traditional battles with the Pawnees and their annual hunting expeditions.

When Little Thunder began leaning more and more on Spotted Tail, it became evident that Spotted Tail was the logical man to succeed Little Thunder's position as chief. The United States Government officials were trying to negotiate treaties from time to time, but an attempted treaty of 1862 failed because no Indians came to negotiate. June 8, 1864 a council was held at Cottonwood. When Little Thunder was too sick to attend, Spotted Tail was delegated to speak for the Brules. Two Strike went with him. The main argument at that time was over hunting and traveling in the Platte Valley. Summer raids on freight trains traveling the overland road on the lower Platte had been most rewarding to the Brules, Cheyenne and Arapaho camps.

Though raiding dwindled in the autumn of 1864, Black Kettle's camp was attacked by Colonel J. M. Chivington of the Colorado volunteers. Vengeance must be made on the whites for the killing of Black Kettle, and Spotted Tail led the Brule operations against the whites. The battle of Julesburg, January 6-7, 1865 on the Platte River was the result, and afterwards Spotted Tail became head chief.

When the Sioux were invited to discuss a treaty at Fort Laramie in June 1866, Spotted Tail led his Brules to Fort Laramie. With them they brought Spotted Tail's young daughter who died on the way to the Fort. The story of Spotted Tail's daughter has been told in many ways, but most of the tales agree that she was a lovely young maiden who had been with Spotted Tail and her mother when they were captive at Fort Leavenworth, and thus had become well acquainted with white military officers. In turn, the white soldiers found her to be worthy of their friendship. Her name has been given variously but probably was either Yellow Buckskin Girl or Wheat Flower. When she realized the gravity of her illness she begged that she be buried at the Fort. Spotted Tail was bringing her body to be buried.

In deference to his wishes, Yellow Buckskin Girl was buried with full military honors, her coffin placed on a gun carriage and followed by her relatives and a group of officers, the troops, and her many Indian friends.

The day after the funeral, the council at Colonel Maynadier's headquarters discussed the signing of a peace treaty. Spotted Tail and Swift Bear remained at Fort Laramie for some weeks, Spotted Tail clearly accepted by the Brules as their leader. When he left he led his people to his camp on the Republican Fork of the river, hunting buffalo and leading a quiet life over the winter. It was the year of the Fort Phil Kearny massacre in the Powder River country, but Spotted Tail was not in that battle. He was learning the ways of the whites, and he was meeting important military officers, peace commissioners from Washington, D. C., generals of the army of the west. In the spring of 1866 Spotted Tail and his friend Swift Bear even had a ride on a Union Pacific train, an event that impressed the two who rode even as much as it awed their Indian friends.

Leavenworth 1858, from *Leslie's*, Dec. 25, 1858. Fort Leavenworth is a few miles north of the city, the spot where Spotted Tail learned the most important lesson of his life. (Photo by courtesy of the Kansas State Historical Society, Topeka)

In 1867 Spotted Tail was issued passes and white flags with the wording "Spotted Tail's Friendly Band," which he carried on hunting expeditions as identification. September 9, Spotted Tail ransomed three white women and three children who had been captured by Cheyennes. He had his reasons for doing so. He brought them to North Platte and presented them to the peace commission September 19.

When the 1868 treaty was signed, Spotted Tail's name was on it. That treaty designated the lands reserved for Sioux occupation, and urged the Sioux to become farmers rather than hunters. Spotted Tail knew that such a change might come eventually, but could not happen because of a few names on a piece of paper. Yet he signed. He was beginning his own brand of battle with the whites through negotiation.

The Brules were ordered to Whetstone Creek near the Missouri River on the theory that their promised annuity goods could be delivered to them by river much easier than to the inland territory. Spotted Tail led his Brules as far as White River thirty to forty miles west of Whetstone Creek, and there he stopped. He knew that agency Indians quickly grew fat, lazy, and could not handle the ever present whiskey. With his band at a distance, short though it might be, Spotted Tail could argue for better rations, more cattle and sometimes he could get it.

The lack of buffalo on the plains by that time made the issuance of cattle to the Indians imperative. The cattle were lean beasts, quick on the hoof. They were turned loose one at a time so the Sioux could chase them and kill them in the old way from the backs of their ponies. It was almost as good as shooting buffalo, and was almost as much fun as a hunt.

In camp Spotted Tail was being recognized as one of the best of the Brule leaders. Many of the Sioux stopped to talk to him and ask his advice. Even the wild Sioux on the Grand River and the Powder River country stopped occasionally. They could see that Spotted Tail could talk with the whites, Spotted Tail could get extra rations by his reasoning power, Spotted Tail had a magic way of speaking that kept the white soldiers in line—and that was something. Gradually many of the Sioux left other bands to join Spotted Tail, and the numbers of his people grew.

He went to Washington several times in the interests of his people. Spotted Tail and Red Cloud were both in the delegation that went east in 1870. While Red Cloud was arguing heatedly against new roads in the west, against military forts on the North Platte river, Spotted Tail was speaking quietly to the officials in an effort to get an agency far from the Missouri River and the right to hunt on the Republican Fork.

From that period of 1870 through the rest of his life, Spotted Tail really became the statesman that made him the greatest chief the Brules ever knew.

He won his fight to get an agency inland. He resisted the efforts of government agents to make farmers of his Brule people because he knew they were not ready for farming, and in spite of everything the government could do Spotted Tail's Brules were not farmers.

When William Welsh, a member of the Board of Indian Commissioners visited Spotted Tail's agency in 1870, Spotted Tail and Swift Bear were visiting the Santee Sioux. When Spotted Tail returned to the Whetstone agency and heard of Welsh's visit, he decided to write Welsh a letter. No Sioux Indian had ever written a letter to be mailed before, and even Spotted Tail did not have enough confidence to do it himself. He dictated it to a white man who had married an Indian woman, and on November 15, 1870, he mailed it. The letter urged Welsh to help in the removal of the Spotted Tail agency to the Upper White River. He knew where he wanted his people to go, a good location on the river bottom that offered water, hunting, trees and grass.

The Brules moved to that location during the winter of 1870-71, but at first it was considered to be merely a Sioux winter camp. Red Cloud's agency was on the north bank of the Platte River west of the Nebraska line and therefore fairly close to Spotted Tail's people. In a spirit of old friendship, the two chiefs joined for a buffalo hunt. Spotted Tail had his people just where he wanted them on a location of his own choosing, hunting when they wanted, free of the Missouri River agencies.

Things were looking good when the Grand Duke Alexis engaged Spotted Tail to help him hunt buffalo. Spotted Tail agreed, and threw into the bargain an entertainment with Indian dancing and feasting. It was quite a party, and the Grand Duke went home happy.

The site of Spotted Tail's agency was not yet official, so in 1872 he went back to Washington to discuss the problem. In Washington, he insisted on removal to a location at the mouth of Beaver Creek on the south bank of White River. Spotted Tail knew the location was quite unfit for farming, a situation that had escaped the white officials' notice. He got his way again, and Agent Risley moved the Brules to that location in 1872.

Spotted Tail, chief of Brules, Sioux tribe, 1868. (Photo from Kingsbury, *History of Dakota Territory*, 1915)

One of Spotted Tail's wives. He had at least four wives. (Bell photo, by courtesy of Adams Memorial Museum, Deadwood)

Skinning a buffalo on the prairie, date around 1870's. Spotted Tail took the Grand Duke Alexis on a buffalo hunt in 1871. (Photo from the collection of S. Goodale Price)

Red Cloud was moved to White River about the same time, and the two Sioux camps were thus only forty miles apart.

Spotted Tail was happy for a short time, though he and Red Cloud were both taking part in the intrigue of Indian agencies, sometimes with success, other times with lesser fortune. Both chiefs recognized that peace with the whites was necessary to the welfare of the Sioux and did their best to keep their people in line. In May 1874 Spotted Tail returned to Washington for further consultation, and not long afterwards his official agency was named on West Beaver Creek near Camp Sheridan, the Spotted Tail Agency.

The year of 1874 gave the Sioux something not quite expected by them. General George Armstrong Custer marched from Fort Abraham Lincoln in northern Dakota Territory with an expedition of 1000 white men and guns, horses, cattle, soldiers, miners, geologists, a photographer and all of their equipage, straight into the hallowed Black Hills in direct contradiction of the 1868 treaty signed by whites and Sioux. Spotted Tail watched, but did nothing until the next year when he heard that another white man, geologist Walter P. Jenney, was being sent into the Black Hills to verify the reports of gold. He invited Agent Howard and twelve head men of his tribe to join him, and led them into the Black Hills to make his own investigation. There was gold in the Black Hills streams. Verifying that, Spotted Tail decided that the Brules should not sell the Black Hills to any white men.

With Spotted Tail's leadership in the matter, when the Sioux were offered six million dollars for the Black Hills the chiefs refused the offer. It was not that simple. Miners were already entering the Black Hills. Towns of tents and slab board homes were springing into being. Gold placering was taking place on the streams.

Spotted Tail's approval was not won by the gift to him of a log house on the first Camp Sheridan site, nor the fact that other Brule chiefs were also given lesser log houses. The Brule women did not know how to take care of a house, and did not care. The houses were a mark of stature, but the Sioux did not live in them.

December 3, 1875 President Grant issued an order for all Sioux to come to the Indian agencies by the end of January or be termed hostiles, the order being issued primarily to the northern Sioux who roamed the plains completely out of control. It was an order that could not be obeyed. The time was the middle of winter and sensible people did not take down their tepees and travel in heavy snow, so the northern Sioux paid no attention to the order.

On the agencies, peace prevailed. In June Spotted Tail visited Fort Laramie where his daughter Yellow Buckskin Girl had been buried. He moved the box containing her bones to his own agency, where the coffin was reburied with ceremony. He was engaged in this and other peaceful pursuits on his agency when the Battle of the Little Big Horn occurred in distant Montana lands. The news of the great battle in which Custer was killed excited the Brules, but Spotted Tail kept his people under quiet control. They had had nothing to do with the death of the yellow haired general. They would do nothing about it now that it was accomplished.

It was about that time that Lieutenant Jesse M. Lee became official military agent at Spotted Tail's Agency, a fact that pleased the chief. Spotted Tail and Lee were close personal friends. There would be no trouble between them.

There was trouble over the Black Hills. The Sioux were ordered to a treaty council, and the treaty was offered to the various chiefs with the information that they must sign or lose their rations. It was a tough demand, but Red Cloud signed the treaty then Spotted Tail signed it for his Brules. There must be peace, and he could see no other way to get it.

In the northern plains, Crazy Horse and Sitting Bull were leading the renegade tribes, the rebellious tribes who would not come to the agencies. There was talk at Camp Robinson and Camp Sheridan, talk on the Spotted Tail Agency and the Red Cloud Agency. General Crook often invited Spotted Tail and Red Cloud to dine with him at Camp Robinson, and the atmosphere on the agencies

Cheyenne Indians skinning beef. Government beef issue was part of a treaty payment to the Indians. (Photo by Grabill 1887)

Indian Sun Dance in Dakota Territory, 1866. (Photo from Armstrong, *The Early Empire Builders of the Great West*)

was one of cooperation although Red Cloud was somewhat cool to Spotted Tail since the latter had been named as chief of both agencies by the white generals. Crazy Horse was making the trouble, and Crazy Horse must be brought to camp.

Spotted Tail agreed to go to Crazy Horse and persuade him to surrender, but only if General Crook would give him a pledge in return that the Oglalas would be treated with liberal terms. He insisted on a strong force of Brule warriors to accompany him, ammunition, rations, supplies, army pack mules to carry his supplies. To cap it all, he asked a promise that the Brules would not be moved to the Missouri River. Crook gave him what he asked, and Spotted Tail left in February 1877 to find Crazy Horse.

He found the great warrior on the Powder River and managed to convince Crazy Horse to lead his people to Camp Robinson where General Crook was waiting for him. Crazy Horse was not difficult to persuade by that time. His own people were tired of flight from white soldiers and hungry on the winter plains, but when he led his people toward the Red Cloud Agency and Camp Robinson they came singing, proud of their Sioux blood, trusting that all would be all right again.

It was not all right. Crazy Horse was at the agency only through the summer when a series of circumstances led to his murder, and the Sioux in his Oglala band were left without a leader. Crazy Horse managed to escort his wife to Spotted Tail's protection before being taken to the Fort Robinson camp, but when he was conducted to the jail there he tried to escape and was killed by a military sword thrust in his body. It was a time of mourning for all Sioux, and a time of mistrust that was heightened when word came that the Sioux would be moved to the Missouri River after all.

Spotted Tail objected. With Red Cloud he made the trip to Washington again to see what they could do. They managed to get only a promise of new negotiations in the spring. October 27, 1877, Spotted Tail led his people from West Beaver Creek towards the east. They would not live on the Missouri River, though they were forced to spend a portion of a winter on its banks in order to get their government annuities of food and clothing.

Two Strike in Washington, 1872, as a member of Spotted Tail's delegation. (From a photograph by Alexander Gardner, by courtesy of the Smithsonian Institution, National Anthropological Archives)

Two Strike and Crow Dog's camp, on Sioux agency, early 1890's. (Photo from the collection of S. Goodale Price)

Chief Spotted Tail, from an oil painting by H. Ulke, 1877. (Photo from the Smithsonian Institution, National Anthropological Archives)

Spotted Tail did not like this at all, and said so with great heat. When Commissioner E. C. Hayt came to the Missouri River to council with the Brules, Spotted Tail made his position plain:

> "We have the promise of the Great Father that we shall be moved to an agency more to our liking in the spring . . . . . We will wait ten days longer, and then if the word of the Great Father is not redeemed, I will bring my young men here, burn these buildings, and move ourselves. I have selected a place for our future home; we are going there, and it is useless for you to say that we shall not go, or that we shall go to some other place." [1]

No directions coming in ten days, Spotted Tail did just what he said he would do. He gave the order to move, and the Brules moved westward to a place Spotted Tail chose on Rosebud Creek in southwestern South Dakota.

A new agent, W. J. Pollock, was appointed to succeed Lieutenant Lee. Pollock did not have the ability to get along with the Brules that Lee had shown, and from the first he was in trouble. The Brules moved where they wanted to move, and were on the Rosebud in strict defiance of government orders, but there they were and there they stayed.

Secretary of the Interior Carl Schurz considered it necessary to pay a personal visit to Spotted Tail in the Rosebud camp. Pollock was released in favor of Agent Cicero Newell, but Spotted Tail recognized Newell immediately as one whom he could manage as easily. He ordered Newell to issue a pass for a Brule to go to Cheyenne River on an errand for him, and Newell did so.

Spotted Tail was beginning to run things to suit himself. When the question appeared of transporting Indian annuities from the Missouri River inland, Spotted Tail's Brules were given the job to haul them by wagon and horses, a job that pleased them to perfection. When Indian Commissioner Schurz ordered Indian police for the Rosebud Agency, Spotted Tail managed to select squaw men or halfbreeds for the job, thus having an ineffectual Indian police band for his people.

Spotted Tail saw the weakness in Agent Newell and began to take over the agency with his own orders. With admirable aplomb, he moved into the agency office and censored the mail from Washington. He ordered Newell to write notes for him to other Indian agents with Brule demands, and Newell did so. He ordered passes for his Indian runners to send word of a Sun Dance by word of mouth, and got them. The Sun Dance was held, in spite of government wrath and astonishment.

Spotted Tail was not exactly in good standing with Washington officials at that time, but when Captain R. H. Pratt of the new Indian training school at Carlisle, Pennsylvania, came to the agency to recruit students, Spotted Tail quickly gained his old prestige when he ordered his own sons and other Brule sons to go for an education. Spotted Tail was not a fool. He recognized the fact that his sons must learn to read and write English in order to be able to negotiate with the white invaders of their lands.

He said, "What we want them to learn is the English language; we want them to be able to read, write and talk in English. If we old folks cannot read nor understand English, we want our children to be able to translate for us the newspapers and tell us what the white people are doing." [2]

Spotted Tail's sons who were sent to Carlisle were Stays at Home (renamed William); Talks With Bear (renamed Oliver); Bugler (renamed Max); Little Scout (renamed Pollock); Running Horse (renamed High Standing Soldier); besides his daughter Red Road and her husband Charles Tackett and Spotted Tail's granddaughter who was the daughter of Black Crow.

While the children were east at Carlisle, life was not exactly quiet on the Rosebud Agency. Rosebud Indian police were ordered to be full bloods, but again Spotted Tail thwarted the intentions of the agent by letting each sub-chief choose his own delegate on the force. Crow Dog, a rebellious Brule chief, was made chief of police, an item that promised trouble for Spotted Tail.

Crow Dog decided to collect range money from white cattlemen who were running cattle on the Indian reservation lands, but found that Spotted Tail was already collecting from them. Spotted Tail was thus one of the first Sioux to realize the value of leasing land to outsiders. Crow Dog was not happy to find that Spotted Tail had the idea before he did, and he began to agitate among his own friends with the idea that Spotted Tail was getting too old to be chief of the Brules any longer.

In January and February Spotted Tail and Red Cloud met together at the Red Cloud Agency on Pine Ridge for a secret conference. While he was gone, the Brules began panning for gold on the flat prairie streams of the Rosebud. Weren't men finding gold in the Black Hills streams? In the excitement Crow Dog was deposed as head police chief, an action making Crow Dog even more unhappy.

Spotted Tail's agent, Cicero Newell, was relieved of his duties at the Rosebud Agency in May, and a new agent, John Cook, arrived. Cook had no idea what was waiting for him. Two traders operated stores on the agency, and for some reason angered Spotted Tail in their methods of trade. The chief sent tribal soldiers and a few Indian police to picket the stores, ordering the Brules to refrain from any purchases until the matter was settled. It was the first time that any Sioux Indian on the plains had thought of picketing, indeed it may have been the first time that anybody at all had thought of picketing a place of business, red man or white man—and credit goes to Spotted Tail for the idea. Agent Cook ordered the pickets to leave, but they refused to listen to Cook. Spotted Tail was their leader, they said.

While Cook was still trying to settle the picketing ordeal, news came to him that Spotted Tail and Red Cloud had refused to cooperate with the railroad being surveyed across the Indian reservations, thus stopping the surveying cold. Summoned, Spotted Tail stated that he was protecting his own people, that was all.

Crow Dog and his supporters began to see how they could oppose Spotted Tail. They could insist that he take orders from the agent. A petition supporting the new agent was signed by Quick Bear, Thunder Hawk, Crow Dog, Brave Bull, Standing Bear and a few other Sioux, presented to Cook and duly filed.

Spotted Tail ignored the petition. In June he was invited with other Brules to attend the first term celebration at Carlisle. He wanted to see how his sons and daughters were doing. When he talked to his sons he learned that they were homesick, in uniform, under stiff discipline and were not being taught to learn English or read or write (the one thing that he had wanted for them) but were being taught farming and carpenter work. He was furious, and announced immediately that he was taking his sons home.

The Secretary of the Interior began to send telegrams to ask him to reconsider, but Spotted Tail did not weaken. He took his four sons, a grandson, a granddaughter and another small boy he claimed as a relative, and went home.

The great majority of the Brules were delighted at this action, but again the opposition party under Crow Dog (reinstated as chief of police) supported the white stand. There was a great argument on the Rosebud, but Spotted Tail refused to send his children back to Carlisle. If they were not taught to read and write, they certainly would not be taught to farm.

The hassle did not deter Spotted Tail's activities in other quarters. He knew his Brule friends better than any agent could. When six Brules stole some horses in Nebraska (a time honored custom) and incidentally killed a white man in the process, Spotted Tail took charge. He persuaded the warriors to submit to arrest,

Spotted Tail and his sons at Carlisle University, June 1880. (Photo by courtesy of the South Dakota State Historical Society)

and then hired a white attorney to defend them—again the first time any Indian thought of pitting white law against white law with appropriate action.

When the attorney demanded payment, Spotted Tail wrote a check. A check on a white man's bank had been beyond the thought of all other Sioux. Spotted Tail did it. If whites could write a check, Spotted Tail could, too. Moreover, he made it stick.

Crow Dog's opposition party was still working. They suggested Yellow Hair as head chief, but the tribal council voted two to one for Spotted Tail. Crow Dog wrote a letter with accusations against Spotted Tail, persuaded three friends to sign it with him, and sent it to the Secretary of the Interior Carl Schurz. Schurz ignored the letter.

Rosebud Agency, about 1885, first called the Spotted Tail Agency. It is located about twelve miles south and west of Mission, South Dakota. It is well worth a side trip to the agency, most of which can be recognized even today from this picture. (Photo by courtesy of the South Dakota State Historical Society)

Crow Dog threatened to shoot Spotted Tail at an Independence Day celebration, but backed down when the opportunity arrived. He did not have the courage to shoot the Brule leader in full view of a crowd. He waited until a better moment—that day of August 5, 1881 when he and his wife were returning to their home after delivering a load of wood.

As they drove along the dusty road they observed four men approaching, Spotted Tail on horseback followed by three sub-chiefs on foot, Two Strike, He Dog and Ring Thunder. Quickly, Crow Dog stopped his team and jumped to the ground, rifle in hand. He knelt as though tieing his moccasin strings, waiting. As Spotted Tail approached, suddenly Crow Dog aimed his rifle at the Brule chief and shot.

Spotted Tail fell from his horse, mortally wounded. He tried to take a step but fell back, dead.

Crow Dog was arrested and taken to the court in Deadwood, South Dakota. By that time a Sioux story had been concocted to the effect that Spotted Tail had made advances toward Crow Dog's wife (some say Medicine Bear's wife), thus Crow Dog was within his right in killing Spotted Tail. Later historians have named this pure poppycock, insisting that the murder was a political plot to unseat Spotted Tail as Brule chief.

The murder succeeded in deposing Spotted Tail, certainly, but it also left the Brules without firm leadership.

Crow Dog remained in Deadwood a short time, was sentenced to hang for the murder, then was temporarily released to take care of his family affairs before his hanging. Before the execution could be performed notification was sent that the Federal Government could not convict an Indian on Indian territory:

> "The first district court of Dakota is without jurisdiction to find or try an indictment for murder committed by one Indian upon another in the Indian country, and conviction and sentence upon such indictment are void and imprisonment thereon is illegal. The Supreme Court of the United States has set aside your conviction." [3]

Crow Dog was released, but he was not a strong enough leader to hold the Brules in line. Spotted Tail's son, Little Spotted Tail (Sintegaleska Chika) tried, but he could not either. White Thunder and Two Strike led separate sections of the Brules for a while, but no man living could take the place of the famous old chief.

Spotted Tail was one of the most brilliant Sioux leaders of his day, or for many years afterwards. He knew and acted on one premise, that in order to protect his Brule people in their old ways he must learn to fight white encroachment with white ways. He could do it because he was able to think one step ahead of the white agents who worked with him. In a day when the red man was only beginning to meet white civilization head on, Spotted Tail stood alone, an outstanding figure of a man who dared to think for himself.

Only recently has his genius been recognized with a monument to Chief Spotted Tail on the Rosebud Reservation, that land chosen by the Brule chief for his people. In 1967 Chauncina Yellow Robe (Mrs. Lee White Horse, Chicago) was selected to unveil the monument. Her father, Chauncey Yellow Robe, was a prominent Sioux leader of the 1920's in Rapid City, South Dakota, himself a member of the Rosebud Sioux and instrumental in leading the Sioux children in modern education with great success. Mrs. White Horse stated in dedicating the monument that such sites help the white people to understand early American history and the Sioux people.

Understand Spotted Tail? Only too well did Spotted Tail understand the whites. Perhaps it is time to give him the honor he deserves.

Quoted References: Spotted Tail, the Strategist.

[1] Kingsbury, George W., *History of Dakota Territory,* Volume I.
    The S. J. Clarke Publishing Company, Chicago, Illinois, 1915. p. 804.
[2] Kingsbury, opus cited, p. 810.
[3] Leedy, Carl, *Black Hills Pioneer Stories.* Bonanza Trails Publishers,
    Lead, South Dakota, 1972.

SITTING BULL,
HUNKPAPA MEDICINE MAN

Sitting Bull, Hunkpapa Sioux, watched the black steam engine puffing on the prairies. The iron horse was hauling more rails to extend the Northern Pacific Railroad farther and farther into the west, into Hunkpapa territory.

Smoke poured from the teakettle chimney of the roaring brute. As it advanced toward a small herd of buffalo the beasts raised their heads in alarm.

Squon-n-n-k! The whistle blew its mournful tone, and the buffalo began to move sluggishly on the tracks, resentful of the thing's intrusion.

"They have no right," Sitting Bull said, and his voice was angry.

The buffalo gave way suddenly. Some crossed the tracks in front of the approaching juggernaut to join their friends. With a flick of their tails they began running, the ground thudding under them. Triumphantly, the black locomotive advanced over the cleared rails, but Sitting Bull was incensed.

"They have no right," he repeated. "This is our land. They did not ask our permission." He paused, and then said with angry jabs of his stick into the ground, "The smoking wagon drives the buffalo from the land—our buffalo which we need for life."

The year was 1870, a period of comparative quiet on the western praries. Two years previously the treaty of 1868 had been signed at Fort Laramie without Sitting Bull's signature, but that treaty had given the lands west of the Missouri River and north of the Platte River, east of the Big Horns and extending to the Canadian border to be Indian reservation lands. It was a big chunk of land, but there were a lot of Sioux scattered over that area and it seemed fair to all.

Now this! A railroad building through that Indian Territory without asking permission of the red men who owned it! Sitting Bull did not ask what his friends thought, he was their leader and he resented the action! It was as he had believed since childhood, the whites could not be trusted to honor their own treaties, and he would tell them so in a manner which they could understand!

Sitting Bull had been born (by his own reckoning, in 1837) near old Fort George on Willow Creek below the mouth of the Cheyenne River, considerably south of the Northern Pacific Railway, but he had moved north with the migration of his Hunkpapa band of Sioux. His father, Jumping Bull, and two uncles, Four Horns and Hunting His Lodge, had been chiefs, which made him eligible for earning such an honor himself. Jumping Bull had been considered rich because of the many ponies he had owned. When Sitting Bull was interviewed in 1881 he said:

> "I have always been running around. Indians that remain on the same hunting grounds all the time can remember years better . . . . I have nine children and two living wives, and one wife that has gone to the Great Spirit. I have two pairs of twins . . . . Was-Seen-By-The-Nation is the name of the old wife. The-One-That-Had-Four-Robes is the name of the other . . . .
>
> "When I was ten years old I was famous as a hunter. My specialty was buffalo calves. I gave the calves I killed to the poor who had no horses. I was considered a good man. My father died twenty one years ago. (1860). For four years after I was ten years old I killed buffalo and fed his people, and thus became one of the fathers of the tribe. At the

TATONKAIYOTONKA, Sitting Bull
The above is a true Photo and Autograph of "Sitting Bull," the Sioux Chief
of the Custer Massacre.

(Photo from the Morrow Collection, by courtesy of the
University of South Dakota Museum)

Sitting Bull, Hunkpapa medicine man. (Photo by
courtesy of the National Archives)

age of fourteen I killed an enemy, and began to make myself great in
battle, and became a chief. Before this, from ten to fourteen, my people
had named me the Sacred Standshoty. After killing an enemy they called me TaTanKa I-You-Tan-Ka, or Sitting Bull. An Indian may be an
inherited chief, but he must make himself a chief by his bravery." [1]

Thus was Sitting Bull's account of his boyhood, but interviews with Indians
show a somewhat different story. It is said that his boyhood name was Slow,
possibly those years before he was ten. The name Sacred Standshoty is interpreted to mean Sacred Stand, and the name Sitting Bull is spelled more often as
Ta-Tan-Ka Yo-Tan-Ka, a spelling which sounds somewhat the same as the one
reported in Sitting Bull's words. Sitting Bull says he earned the name by killing
an enemy, though another story says he acquired the name when he was sitting
astride a buffalo bull to skin the animal, believing it dead, when the buffalo got to
his feet in a determined effort to live. A photo exists purporting to show Sitting
Bull and his ninth wife, which is more than the three wives of whom he spoke.
    Be that as it may, Sitting Bull was a hunter in his youth, and he didn't always
hunt buffalo. He resented the white encroachment, and delighted in harassing the
military men whenever possible. He was said by his Indian friends to be more of a

Railroad train encountering a herd of buffalo in crossing the plains, Dakota Territory. Sitting Bull was angered at the building of the Northern Pacific across Indian Territory in 1870. (Photo of painting by Ernest Gricer, from the collection of S. Goodale Price)

medicine man than a warrior, but he was a leader. He had a powerful persuasion, and he played on the superstitions of his people with adept imagination. When Sitting Bull spoke, Hunkpapas listened.

He took immediate action against the whites when he saw the Northern Pacific pushing through his lands in northern Dakota Territory. With small raids followed by loyal Hunkpapas, Sitting Bull made nuisance attacks wherever he could. As the year continued the raids became more than nuisance. They were downright obnoxious.

In a report from General D. S. Stanley at Fort Sully dated July 1, 1871, Stanley said:

> "When the Northern Pacific Railroad crosses the Missouri, the entire Sioux question will be brought to a head, and in my opinion will only be solved by an Indian war of some magnitutde." [2]

Stanley named fragments of Santee, Yanktonnais and Sissetons who had joined Sitting Bull's leadership in the forays against the whites.

The military men knew at the time that they were dealing with two Sioux chiefs named Sitting Bull. The Hunkpapa Sitting Bull was their adversary, cunning, resentful, becoming more and more powerful. Sitting Bull the Oglala was a man of a different stripe altogether, a Sioux chief whose greatest wish was to help the whites in their efforts to bring an honorable peace to the plains. The Oglala Sitting Bull lived on Red Cloud Agency, and he did what he could to ease the tensions between whites and red men. He was welcomed in Washington, D. C. with other Sioux chiefs on delegations to meet President Grant, and was killed by Crow Indians while leading a party of six Indians to negotiate with the United States representatives. Let it be clearly understood then, the man whom we discuss in this book is Sitting Bull, the Hunkpapa, medicine man, orator, chief and leader of his people whether or not he can be proved to have been a warrior of any stature or not.

Sitting Bull, Hunkpapa, was still opposing the rails of the Northern Pacific in every way possible by 1873, having given two good years to the job. Still the rails went forward. Commisssioner of Indian Affairs E. P. Smith made a tour of the Indian agencies in the northwest that summer, and though he is said to have penetrated even as far as Sitting Bull's camp, apparently he was not able to pacify the Hunkpapa leader. Smith met a friendly attitude among most of the Indian tribes, but still Sitting Bull had to be recognized for what he was—the foremost uncompromising opponent of all treaties of cession and continued construction of the railroad. He was supported by a growing force of determined warriors from several tribes. He was a man to be carefully considered.

Nevertheless Sitting Bull was not always in search of the white man's scalp. McGillycuddy, agent for the Red Cloud reservations, mentioned that Sitting Bull and a small group of hunters approached a military expedition on the Marias River in Montana in 1874 and asked peacefully if the soldiers had seen buffalo.

Sitting Bull identified himself proudly, "How kola. Mea Ta-Ton-ka Yo-ton-ka." [3]

McGillycuddy said that they gave the Indian band some sacks of tobacco and

"after much handshaking and friendly grunts of How kola, Sitting Bull's hunting party rode off." [4]

Powder River, Wyoming, at Interstate 90, from the east bank, 1971. The Sioux hostiles roamed around the Powder River country in the 1870's, including Sitting Bull and his warriors. (Photo by Fielder)

Regardless of Sitting Bull's occasional lapses into friendliness, he never went to a treaty council. His name was never found signed to any white treaty, and he continued to resent the white attitude that red men would sign away their rightful land. By that time his home was north of the border between South and North Dakota (though the two states were not yet divided as such) in the area which later became known as the Standing Rock Agency.

Events were quickening for both red and white man. When in 1874 General George A. Custer led an exploratory party into the Black Hills, Sitting Bull knew of it as soon as the word flashed across the prairies. The military men had violated the Fort Laramie 1868 treaty again in even marching into the Black Hills region. Geologist Walter P. Jenney led another expedition into the forbidden Black Hills the next summer, and Sitting Bull organized a war party. His plans were somewhat nebulous, so his hatred first took the form of sniping bullets into military camps at night.

They could not catch him. He led his warriors in cunning surprise and run tactics that did nothing as far as winning a war was concerned, but the soldiers knew he was there.

The order from President Grant in December 1875 ordering all Indians to reservations by January 31, 1876 did little more than anger Sitting Bull to new

Cheyenne warriors in council costume. Sioux from various tribes joined Sitting Bull at different times. The Cheyennes were also at the Battle of the Little Big Horn. (Photo from the Morrow collection, by courtesy of the University of South Dakota Museum)

heights of contempt. To expect him to lead the Hunkpapa band across the deep snows and freezing winds of the northern prairies in the dead of winter was an idiot's dream! He ignored the suggestion, but he filed it in his mind to add to the other insults which he had harbored through the years.

With the first warm days the armies of both Indians and whites were on the march. The Sioux of the northern plains including Hunkpapas, Cheyennes, Minneconjous, Sans Arc and Oglalas were meeting in the greatest gathering of Sioux people in many years. It was a joyous occasion at first, friends meeting friends after long absences from one another. The great Indian camp lay spread along a bank of the Little Big Horn for three miles up and down the river.

While the Sioux were moving together, General Terry had his own instructions. The wild Sioux of the north had ignored the President's order to come to the reservations, and Terry was one of the generals assigned the job of bringing them there. Scouts had reported seeing the immense Indian camp, and Terry made his plans. He sent a column under General Gibbon up the Yellowstone River toward the Tongue River. He ordered General Custer up Rosebud Creek to follow a broad Indian trail. They would catch the Sioux between them, and it should be an easy victory.

So they thought, but Sitting Bull was doing a little planning of his own. If Terry's scouts had seen the Sioux village, Sitting Bull's scouts had the information on the approach of the bluecoats as quickly. Sitting Bull called a war council. Hunkpapa warriors with him included Gall, Crow King and Black Moon. The great warrior Crazy Horse headed the Oglalas with Low Dog and Big Road. Two Moon and White Bull led the northern Cheyennes. Hump was there with his Minneconjous, and Spotted Eagle spoke for the Sans Arc. Rain in the Face was there from another tribe.

Sectional view of Sitting Bull's Camp. (Photo from the Morrow collection, by courtesy of the University of South Dakota Museum)

Sioux Squaws captured from Sitting Bull, 1877. This was a year after the Battle of the Little Big Horn. (Photo from Kingsbury, ''History of Dakota Territory,'' 1915)

Issuing rations, April 18, 1882. An Indian with a pipe in hand in the foreground watching the artist, some officers and their families with Indians standing and squatting around them. Behind them the camp, and in the distance (not visible in the photo) are hills covered with snow. (Photo from the Morrow Collection, by courtesy of the University of South Dakota Museum)

Most historians agree that Crazy Horse and Gall led the fighting Indians into the Battle of the Little Big Horn, but Sitting Bull planned the attack. Crazy Horse is also given credit by some as being one of the finest tacticians in prairie warfare of those years, so it is possible that he too had a word in the planning and certainly had the most powerful hand in the execution. When the Battle of the Little Big Horn was finished, Custer and the Seventh Cavalry were dead, and the Indians were running fron Terry, Reno, Gibbon and the rest of the army.

Though reports of their activities were given later by Major Reno and other soldiers under his and Benteen's command, only two eye witness stories were related by Indian warriors who were in the battle which killed Custer, those made by Sitting Bull and by his chief warrior Gall many years later.

Sitting Bull told his story to the Reverend J. B. M. Genin, Catholic missionary to the Sioux, who gave it to the North Dakota Historical Collections, later published by George W. Kingsbury:

" 'We knew the soldiers were coming upon us weeks before the fight, yet we did not want to fight if we could do otherwise. In our camp on the Little Big Horn there were the tribes of the Tetons as follows: The Uncpapas, who had many lodges. The Santees, with many warriors, whose lodges were pitched next to the Uncpapas. Next came the lodges of the Oglala—not so many. The Brule (Sisphi) Sioux came next in the order of their tepees. The Minneconjou lodges were next. The Sans Arc lodges were pitched next. The Blackfeet lodges came next. The Cheyenne camp came next. There were some Arickaree Indians in the camp with some of the Sioux tribe, and some of the Two Kettle tribe also, these being visitors and without lodges of their own.

" 'We did not go out there to fight. We took along our women and children, and went to meet all the tribes of this region, to make laws and treaties and to visit each other, and to make our young men and maidens acquainted with each other, so they could marry, as our fathers have done for many generations. So, when we found the white soldiers were following us, we marched back into the hills a long way, still being pursued by the army in direct violation of the treaty of 1868, which article first pledges the honor of the United States to keep peace. We resolved to camp and wait the will of God, at the same time praying to God to save us from the hands of our enemies, now near, and coming without provocation to complete our extermination.

" 'For three days our scouts watched Custer marching toward our camp. I therefore sent all our women and children into places of safety through the low lands. We expected the soldiers would charge through the village, as they did at the battle of Washita in 1868, when Chief Black Kettle was killed, and the women and children trampled to death under the hoofs of their war horses. The Teton Indians are too brave and love their families too well to let them be butchered even by the soldiers of the United States, and not fight for them until death.

" 'So I sent my young men to light fires inside and outside the deserted tepees, placing conveniently at the door of each of the front tepees sticks dressed like men, and to put up stakes in the front streets of the village, to which were tied pieces of blankets, so that when the fires were burning fiercely, and stirring the air, the pieces of cloth and old rags waved to and fro in the breeze and gave the appearance of a densely populated village. Then I marched behind the front row of hills with all my braves, and awaited the opening of the soldiers' fire upon our camp. Everything worked as I had planned. True to their intentions, the United States soldiers killed my flagmen whom I had sent to meet them and demand peace, and proceeding furiously forward, opened fire upon my empty camp of old tepees and rag manikins. I

Sioux chiefs Two Strike, Crow Dog, and High Hawk. (Photo by courtesy of South Dakota Historical Society)

Sitting Bull, Hunkpapa medicine man. (Photo from the collection of S. Goodale Price)

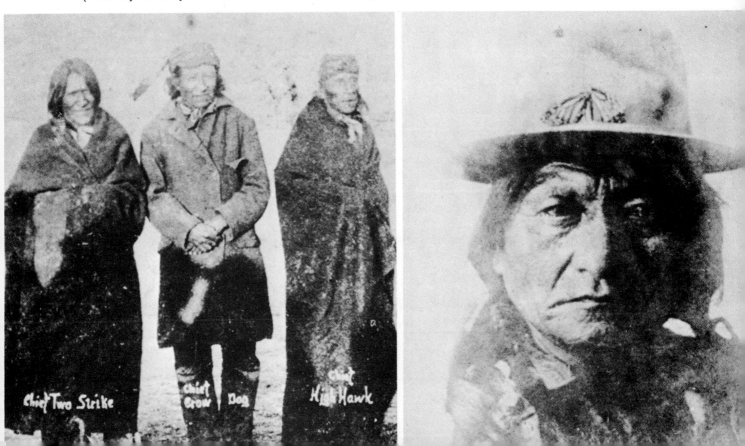

Chief Two Strike Chief Crow Dog High Hawk

Sitting Bull, Squaw, and Twins. This is his last wife. She is number 9, age 29, and has six children three of whom are shown in this view. The youngest one, on her back, is one year old, and the twins, five years old, are sitting one on each side of "Little Bell." (Photo from the Morrow Collection, by courtesy of the University of South Dakota Museum)

then fell upon them from the rear, with all my force, before they had time to recover from the shock of their furious charge and their surprise at finding the village deserted. My men destroyed the last of them in a very short time. Now they accuse me of slaying them. Yet what did I do? Nothing. God saved our lives because we had called upon him. They should then accuse God, for truly it was he who saved us by permitting them to die.

" 'It was very hard to place any faith in the word of Americans. Ever since I knew them my experience with them has proved that they continually cheat the Indians, over-reaching upon their lands with big promises, never fulfilled, and at last finding some pretext to kill them.

" 'These soldiers were not brave. When they saw our warriors they ran away as fast as they could and hid in the hollows of the hills. I was not in that part of the battlefield. I sat on my horse on a hill and sent my young men to direct the movements of the head warriors. All my warriors were brave and knew no fear. The soldiers who were all killed were brave men, too, but they had no chance to fight or run away; they were surrounded too closely by our many warriors. As they stood there waiting to be killed, they were seen to look far away to the hills in all directions, and we knew they were looking for the hidden soldiers in the hollows of the hills to come and help them. But our warriors first killed the soldiers who were holding the horses and rode them while

Indians with Buffalo Bill's Wild West Show, Chicago, 1893. Sitting Bull was part of the show in 1885. (Photo by courtesy of the Nebraska State Historical Society)

charging close up and firing at the survivors. Let no man call this a massacre. It was a piece of mere warfare. We did not go out of our own country to kill them. They came to kill us and got killed themselves. God so ordered it.

" 'I did not kill the Yellow Hair. He was a fool and rode to his death.'

"He said further that he did not personally see General Custer during the battle; that his people searched for the body of the long haired white chief after the battle, but that no soldier with long hair was found. Sitting Bull further said that when all of General Custer's men had been killed his warriors rushed to surround the soldiers on the hill with Reno, and that they would have soon killed them, too, but a false alarm was raised that some soldiers had escaped and were attacking the women and children, and the whole Indian army surged in that direction. Then when the mistake was found out, and his command surged again to the hill where Reno's men were concealed, he gave the order that there should be no more fighting. 'We have killed enough,' he said. 'Let the rest go back and take care of the women and children, and tell the people how the Indians can fight. Whereat his warriors were sorrowful and wanted to kill all Reno's men, and then go to give battle to the 'walking soldiers' (Terry's infantry) when they should leave the steamboat, but they obeyed his orders although greatly disappointed."[5]

General Terry's soldiers were seen coming across the prairie, and the entire Indian gathering moved up the river toward the Big Horn Mountains. The battle was finished.

Crazy Horse took his Oglalas into hiding around the Powder River country. The Sioux broke into many small bands, but Sitting Bull and Gall led three or four hundred warriors north with all haste into British Columbia and the safety of Canada where he lived peacefully until July 1881. There were sometimes

Sitting Bull and Buffalo Bill Cody. (Photo by courtesy of the Nebraska State Historical Society)

rumors that Sitting Bull was leading a war party into Black Hills towns, creating all kinds of apprehension to the miners placering the streams, but they were only rumors. Siting Bull was in Canada, and there he remained for over four years.

During that time the Red Cloud Agency at Pine Ridge and the Spotted Tail Agency on the Rosebud were areas of peace. True, there had been a bad time when Crazy Horse led his Oglalas to surrender at Fort Robinson, and four months later met death at the point of a bayonet rather than be imprisoned in the white man's jail, but the Sioux were beginning to recognize that their main chance for survival lay in cooperation with the whites who were coming to the western prairies in ever increasing numbers.

In 1879 an Oglala chief, Young Man Afraid of His Horses, gave an impassioned speech in which he emphasized that the Sioux on reservations wanted to get along with the white soldiers and the Great Father. He said:

> "All the bad Indians are now in the north with Sitting Bull . . . some young men have joined Sitting Bull who would never have done so had their chiefs been young men like most of the Oglalas at the Pine Ridge Agency . . . ." [6]

And there sat Sitting Bull in Canada, waiting.

He might have held his fortress longer if the buffalo had lasted, but they did not. As the frontier advanced westward the large buffalo herds were gradually decimated, and as the buffalo disappeared Sitting Bull's people found themselves increasingly hungry.

Sitting Bull and his chief henchman, Gall, quarrelled. Gall challenged Sitting Bull's counsel of annihilation of all whites, saying that the Hunkpapas must

50

recognize the need for cooperation between the two people. When Sitting Bull retorted angrily, Gall left, taking with him many warriors. Sitting Bull's people heard that Gall surrendered on January 3, 1881.

Finally Sitting Bull decided that he had had enough. In May 1881 he sent a messenger to General Hazen at Fort Buford with a message asking the terms of his surrender. Hazen stated that he would accept unconditional surrender with the requirement that the Indians give up all their arms and ponies. Small groups straggled into the fort after that, and July 20, 1881 Sitting Bull himself arrived. He voluntarily surrendered to Major Brotherton, the commander.

Sitting Bull and his people were put on board a steamboat and transported to Fort Yates at the Standing Rock Agency. At Bismarck the party halted briefly, and it was discovered that Sitting Bull could write his name. Autograph hunters besieged him. He obliged them with his signature, enjoying the attention which he received.

When they arrived at Fort Yates he was given quarters with several thousand other Indians who were gathered there. As time passed, the presence of growing numbers of Sioux at Fort Yates suggested that it would be better to move Sitting Bull to Fort Randall down the Missouri River some miles. Sitting Bull protested, but the steamboat came. He was escorted upon it, and once again he moved. He was kept under close surveillance for about a year, then released in 1883 and returned to his old lands on the Grand River close to the Standing Rock Agency.

During his stay at Fort Randall a German artist, Dr. Rudolf Cronau, visited the fort and became acquainted with Sitting Bull. Indeed, he painted his portrait, and in doing so managed to talk to the chief about various affairs. Sitting Bull told him the "sad history of his people," [7] Dr. Cronau said, in which he described the miserable ways that he had been treated by the United States Government.

> "For several weeks I remained at Fort Randall, and often enjoyed Sitting Bull's sympathetic company. At such times he tried to improve my knowledge of the Dakota language, while he made efforts to learn German." [8]

Sitting Bull was beginning to accept the white people as possible friends. Learning German language? It was a whole new way of life for the old renegade. He had not been able to admit anything good of the white people, but there he was sitting for a portrait and learning a white man's language!

By 1885 he had quieted his animosities towards the whites so greatly that when the world famous Buffalo Bill Cody approached him with an invitation to join his Wild West Show, it didn't take much persuasion. He toured the United States and several foreign countries with the Wild West Show. Buffalo Bill billed him as "Enemies in '75, friends in '85." [9] The Wild West Show presented Indian war dances, bucking bronchos and a western rodeo, buffaloes and a simulated prairie fire, even an Indian village with a sham battle between Indian tribes. It was a great success, particularly in London where they played for British royalty.

In 1888 President Grover Cleveland summoned Sitting Bull, Gall and John Grass to Washington to discuss making the Standing Rock Agency a permanent fixture of government. Sitting Bull opposed the reduction of land in the treaty. Gall and Grass supported the terms. If Gall and Sitting Bull had quarreled before, they became bitter enemies when the Standing Rock Agency was established in 1889.

Sitting Bull was there at Standing Rock when the Messiah craze began.

In 1890 reports began to filter over the western plains that the Messiah had returned to rescue the Indians from their plight. Word was that the Messiah lived in the mountains of Nevada, and that he would restore the Indian hunting grounds to the red man, bring the buffalo back to the prairies, and all the dead Indians would come to life again. The Messiah was actually a full blooded Paiute Indian named Wavoka, Hopkins, Jack Wilson, the Red God of Nevada, and names that white military men called him under their breath.

Wavoka may have believed the story himself. He had had visions and had swooned into unconsciousness during the time of the eclipse of the sun. Wavoka also knew magic tricks, having traveled with a magician for a time.

Whatever Wavoka's magic may have been, the marvels that he offered his brother red men caught their imagination with fire. Three Sioux from the southern Dakota Territory agencies, Kicking Bear, Short Bull and Porcupine, journeyed to Nevada to meet the Messiah, but so secretly that their agents did not even know of their absence until months after they returned. They did return, and with them additional news of the marvelous powers of the Messiah.

The natural way for Indians to observe religious ceremonies had always been by dancing, so in the Messiah dream of salvation the Indians were given a dance to show their belief in the coming of the Messiah. To protect themselves, they were given ghost shirts which would keep the bullets of white men's guns from killing them. They began to dance.

This was just the kind of stuff that Sitting Bull had been practicing all his life. Though he had been living a semi-retired life of quietness since his days with the Buffalo Bill Wild West Show, the old grudges against the white pioneers were still burning in his mind. According to the General Nelson A. Miles' narrative as retold by Kingsbury:

> "The information aroused the old time belligerent nature of Sitting Bull and stirred to life his smouldering ambition to free his country from the presence of the white race. He declared that they would not wait for the coming of the Messiah but organize and go forth to meet him. He sent out runners to every tribe in the northwest that he knew of, and also to Canadian tribes, appealing to them to rise and leave their reservations, assemble near the base of the Rocky Mountains, and march west until they should meet with the Messiah, and escort him on this crusade of deliverance."[10]

Miles called Sitting Bull,

> "the great organizer and controlling spirit of the hostile element. None of the other Indians possessed the power of drawing and molding the hearts of his people to one purpose . . . ." [11]

Knowing that Sitting Bull was quite capable of influencing the entire Sioux nation to his way of thinking, when General Miles heard of Sitting Bull's complete endorsement of the Messiah and the plan to escort the Messiah toward the great encampment of Indians, Miles worried. It had not been long enough to forget the great village of Sioux that had routed and killed Custer and the Seventh Cavalry. Indian emotion could be whipped to a frenzy, Miles had seen it happen. Reports said that the Messiah meeting would be in the Bad Lands of South Dakota east of the Black Hills.

General Miles considered it necessary to stop Sitting Bull immediately before he could lead his force of two hundred followers toward either the Messiah or the Bad Lands. He issued orders to the commanding officer at Fort Yates to arrest Sitting Bull. Major E. G. Fechet was given a command of a troop of cavalry and 42 Indian police. According to Miles' own account:

"Major Fechet moved his camp at night some thirty miles to a close proximity to Sitting Bull's camp, and sent his friendly Indians forward to arrest the notorious war chief. These friendlies proceeded to Sitting Bull's lodge and informed him that he was a prisoner and must go with them. He protested, but without avail. They had proceeded but a few steps when he uttered the war cry, which aroused his followers, who rushed to rescue him. Then occurred a short, desperate combat in which Sitting Bull was killed, with quite a number of his followers, as well as five of the Indians who made the arrest." [12]

The day was December 15, 1890. Sitting Bull was dead. His son Crowfoot, who had urged Sitting Bull to resist arrest, was killed. Beside them thirteen Sioux warriors lay dead, too. It had been a tragic day.

Sitting Bull's people fled the camp when they saw Fechet's troops approaching. The body of Sitting Bull was taken to Standing Rock Agency and Fort Yates, where it was said that it was buried secretly with quickline over the remains.

Many years later Mrs. Mary Long Chase, daughter of the man who killed Sitting Bull, Lieutenant Bullhead, spoke of the occasion with sadness:

"My father was ordered to bring Sitting Bull in dead or live. He wanted to bring him in alive, but the foolishness of the ghost dancers caused the fight." [13]

The Bad Lands, South Dakota. Big Foot led his Minneconjous and the Sitting Bull people into the Bad Lands after Sitting Bull's death in 1890. (Photo by Fielder, 1965)

The body of Big Foot, dead on the battlefield at Wounded Knee, December 1890. (Photo from the collection of S. Goodale Price)

The frozen bodies of Indian dead after the Battle of Wounded Knee, December 1890. The inscription written at the bottom of the picture states that this is the Indian who fired the first shot, but reputable historians say that no one person was identified as the first man to shoot. (Photo from the collection of S. Goodale Price)

In any case, the result of Sitting Bull's murder led directly to the Battle of Wounded Knee, the last great confrontation between white men and red men.

Chief Big Foot, a lesser but capable chief, had led his band of Minneconjous to the south fork of the Cheyenne River, to continue their ghost dancing, and a battalion of the Eighth Cavalry intercepted him to arrest the entire group. Big Foot told Colonel E. V. Sumner that he was going to Fort Bennett and Cheyenne Agency to collect food rations for his people. Sumner believed him, and let him go.

The fugitives from the Sitting Bull killing met Big Foot not long afterwards, and with the telling of the story Big Foot became alarmed. He led his people into the Bad Lands to escape the soldiers, but was recaptured by Major Whiteside and a battalion of the Seventh Cavalry. Big Foot had contracted pneumonia in the flight. Sick, tired, he surrendered and hoisted a white flag over his tent. With the cavalry as escort, Big Foot and his people were conducted to a point at Wounded Knee and guns placed on a hill surrounding the Indian camp to keep them in line.

The next morning the soldiers demanded that all Indian guns be given to them in complete surrender. To make sure that they got them they began a systematic search for weapons. Nobody knows for sure who fired the shot that touched off the slaughter, whether Indian or soldier, but with the firing of that shot pandemonium flared. The white soldiers began firing into the Indian camp, shooting at anything that moved. When the panic subsided, nearly three hundred men, women and children of Chief Big Foot's band, including Big Foot himself, and between thirty and forty troopers were killed.

If Sitting Bull's death had been a tragic mistake, this was a worse one. The dead were buried in mass graves, and the living mourned.

In 1953 Sitting Bull's remains came into the news again in a startling manner. His descendants asked for permission to move the body to South Dakota from his North Dakota grave, on the basis that Sitting Bull had been born in South Dakota and therefore should be buried in that state. Since the request was sixty three years after Sitting Bull's death, it was denied.

Thereupon a nephew of Sitting Bull and a group of his friends robbed the grave (or so they claimed) and reburied whatever was left of Sitting Bull near the Missouri River at Mobridge, South Dakota, a few miles west of the Grand River. Then they poured twenty tons of concrete on top the grave to keep the bones from being moved again.

Remembering the report that quicklime had been buried with Sitting Bull's body, it is hardly likely that any bones were left, but that was the story released to the newspapers in 1953. Korczak Ziolkowski, whose immense statue of Crazy Horse is being carved in the Black Hills at this time, constructed a six ton statue of Sitting Bull to place on top the Mobridge grave, and there it remains—Sitting Bull's grave in South Dakota.

He was a powerful leader. He may not have been any kind of a warrior at all—indeed his own Indian friends disclaim any pretence of Sitting Bull's ever being a warrior—but the man had a fighting personality that drew followers to his projects like iron filings to a magnet. If Sitting Bull spoke for war, he had warriors waiting to perform for him. It was as simple as that.

Sitting Bull acted as he sincerely believed. That his belief was contrary to the needs of the times makes him no less a man of stature, a man who will be remembered in history.

Quoted References: Sitting Bull, Hunkpapa Medicine Man.

[1] Kingsbury, George W., *History of Dakota Territory.* The S. J. Clarke Publishing
    Company, Chicago, 1915. Volume I, pp. 825, 826.

[2] Kingsbury, opus cited, pp. 767, 768.

[3] McGillycuddy, Julia B., *McGillycuddy: Agent.* Stanford University Press,
    Stanford, California, 1941, p. 19.

[4] McGillycuddy, opus cited, p. 20.

[5] Kingsbury, opus cited, pp. 965, 966.

[6] "Let The Young Men Rule Was Plea of Sioux Chief," *Rapid City Journal,*
    September 28, 1969. Rapid City, South Dakota.

[7] Cronau, Dr. Rudolf, "My Visit Among the Hostile Dakota Indians and How
    They Became My Friends," *South Dakota Historical Collections,* Volume XXII.
    South Dakota State Historical Society, Pierre, South Dakota, 1946. p. 417.

[8] Cronau, opus cited, p. 417.

[9] Dancker, Dorothy, "Sitting Bull Still Controversial Figure 75 Years After His Death,"
    Rapid City Journal, December 14, 1965. Rapid City, South Dakota.

[10] Kingsbury, opus cited, p. 827.

[11] Kingsbury, opus cited, p. 828.

[12] Kingsbury, opus cited, p. 827.

[13] "Aged Indian Woman Recalls Why Dad Shot Sitting Bull," *Rapid City
    Daily Journal,* April 12, 1953. Rapid City, South Dakota.

GENERAL CUSTER'S EXPEDITION ON THE MARCH.

The Custer expedition of 1874 on its march to the Black Hills. (Photo drawn from one of Illingworth's photos, by courtesy of the South Dakota State Historical Society)

4

GALL, RENO'S OPPONENT

Gall faced the white men, his head high and defiant. He held his fur robe around him. He carried his rifle. He had not wanted to talk to the government commissioners but they had come to him at Fort Rice on the Missouri River on July 2, 1868, and demanded that he speak.

He spoke, his voice grim:

"I have been driven from one gulch to another, to mountains and plains, far from home by your soldiers. I have been hunted, hounded, and wounded by them." [1]

With a swift passion he flung his fur robe to the floor. Standing only in his moccasins and breechclout, every eye in the circle of the men was focused on a great red stripe of blood that crossed his chest, the blood still dripping down his side and leg.

"My wounds have not yet healed, and I am not ready to take you by the hand and call you friend . . . Many of these men before me were at the treaty of Fort Laramie. The promises the Great Father made were utterly false. He told us one thing and did another." [2]

Gall turned his magnificent physique until he was looking directly at General William S. Harney, and continued:

"If we kill a bad white man who molests us, we are hounded until we have paid with twenty lives for one . . . . Your hands are red with blood, you see the bleeding wounds on my breast . . . . Not until this fort is burned down and I can see my foot prints in the dead ashes will I believe what you say. Not until the wounds I carry are healed, the lands that belong to us restored, will I sign a treaty with you." [3]

He meant it.

Long years afterwards, he changed his mind.

As long as he could remember he had fought with the Hunkpapa warriors and with his boyhood friend, Sitting Bull, against the continued movement of white men into Indian lands.

Gall had been born around 1838 possibly a year or two younger than Sitting Bull. Though Sitting Bull had been the son of chiefs, Gall was the son of nobody of distinction. Gall was a fighter from the time he could lift an arrow, and because of his fighting ability he needed only himself to prove that he was a great man in the Hunkpapa tribe of Sioux. His name Pizi meant The Gall, and he remained Gall through his lifetime.

He began to get the attention of military men as early as 1866 when frontier campaigners, recognizing their repeated adversary, called him "the fighting cock of the Sioux." [4] Fighting cock was a mild term. Gall fought, and wounds did not stop him. He caught the bullet in his chest in a fight November 25, 1867, but had ignored the wound as much as he could.

Gall, Hunkpapa warrior chief. (Photo from Kingsbury, *History of Dakota Territory*, 1915)

He refused to go to Fort Laramie for the 1866 peace talks. Though his November wound still bothered him, he went to the conference in April 1868 at Fort Laramie, hoping that something good would come of the treaty. Angry at the way things progressed, he left to follow Red Cloud into war on the Bozeman Trail. His signature was not on that 1868 treaty. In an effort to persuade the fighting warrior to reconsider, the commissioners found Gall at Fort Rice, but it was a useless attempt.

When the conference ended, Gall left. In his anger he led a group of warriors in attacking Fort Buford. It was a disastrous battle for him. He took a couple of bullets from the white soldiers and lay helpless on the battlefield until his friends carried him from the scene. He had a tough body, and he managed to recover from his new wounds.

Histories of Indian battles with the whites seem to be slanted one way or another, either showing the Indian as a noble red man who was vastly discriminated against by cruel white soldiers, or reporting the soldiers as men doing their duty in trying to protect innocent white emigrants from a savage lustful red man who had no idea of dealing reasonably with the whites. The truth is that there were two sides, the Indians' and the whites', and both were as much to blame as the other.

The Sioux saw their lands disappearing as the white emigrants approached, and fought in every way they knew to save their ancestral hunting grounds. The soldiers saw their own people being scalped, burned, captured, tortured by primitive savages, and fought as furiously and as barbarously as the red man because they had to do so for their lives.

After the treaty of 1868 there was comparative quiet on the western frontier until the Northern Pacific Railway started pushing its rails across the Indian territory in northern Dakota in 1870 and Sitting Bull began retaliating in raids against the whites. Gall had become Sitting Bull's chief warrior, the right hand fighter upon whom Sitting Bull depended for leadership on the field. Wherever Sitting Bull led the Sioux warriors, be they from Hunkpapa tribes or others, Gall was there, ready and willing to fight.

The years gathered momentum. The rails were still moving westward in 1871, 1872, 1873, and Sitting Bull and Gall could not stop them. In 1874 General George Custer led an expedition of a thousand men into the Black Hills, an area smack-dab in the middle of the Indian territory designated in the 1868 treaty. The next year Walter P. Jenney and his men went into the Black Hills, and little groups of mining men began filtering into the hills from all directions.

There was no stopping the gold rush into the hills, but the Sioux did not like this unpermitted entry into their lands. The President's order issued December 3, 1875 that all Sioux move to recognized agencies by January 31, 1876, was an effort to control the Sioux harassment, but it was a poor time to make such a proclamation. The month was the cold of winter. No Sioux in his right mind would pay attention to such foolishness, and the roving bands of northern Sioux, Hunkpapas or Oglalas or any of the others, ignored the order.

A week after the expiration date the Secretary of the Interior and the General of the Army ordered Lt. General Philip H. Sheridan to bring the Indians to the agencies.

In the spring of 1876 three military expeditions moved from different directions toward the heart of hostile Indian country on the Powder River and Little Big Horn areas. Brigadier General George Crook started his troops from Fort Fetterman, Wyoming, moving north. General Alfred H. Terry, Commander of the northern operations, sent General John Gibbon's cavalry from Fort Ellis, Montana, and infantry from Fort Shaw, Montana, to march east down the Yellowstone River. General Terry left Fort Abraham Lincoln in present North

Buffalo in Custer State Park, Black Hills, South Dakota. Buffalo were a necessity to Indian life when the Sioux were roaming the western prairies, and their decimation was one reason the Sioux resented the coming of the white people. (Photo by Donald Blair)

Major Marcus A. Reno. (Photo by courtesy of the South Dakota State Historical Society)

Captain F. W. Benteen (Photo by courtesy of the South Dakota State Historical Society)

Dakota lands on May 17, 1876 with two companies of the Seventeenth Infantry, one company of the Sixth Infantry, and the Seventh Cavalry under General George A. Custer. The three were to meet on hostile country, hoping to trap the enemy Indians between them and bring them to heel.

Indian scouts knew of the movements of the whites from the beginning, and Gall was eager for battle. He joined Crazy Horse's warriors when Sitting Bull was not yet ready to give orders to fight. When Crazy Horse caught General Crook's troops on the Rosebud Creek, June 17, Gall was believed to have been Crazy Horse's second in command.

There was blood in the air, and the Sioux were ready for anything.

When the battle with Crook was finished, Crazy Horse and Gall jubilantly turned their horses and their men toward the north, ready to join their friends.

On the banks of the Little Big Horn several tribes of Sioux from the northern prairies were gathering in one of the biggest encampments that had been known for many years. According to Sitting Bull's later account of the Battle of the Little Big Horn, the immense congregation of Indian tribes at the Little Big Horn was not meant to be there for war. Rather, Sioux had gathered for an annual festive occasion, friends meeting friends, young men and young women being brought together to meet and marry. They fought the white men, Sitting Bull said, because the soldiers followed them and would not let them stay in peace.

Twelve to fifteen thousand Sioux in one big camp made problems for themselves as well as the whites. Their huge herd of horses quickly ate the available grass, making it imperative to move to new ground unless they wanted their horses at a distance from the camp which would not be easy to guard. Still, they must be near water.

On June 24, 1876, the Sioux lodges moved across the Little Big Horn in an orderly procession directed by a herald, and by evening they were encamped in the new spot where there was fresh grass for their horses and a better camping spot for the people. That night the Sioux danced for the sheer fun of being together, and on the prairies a short distance away, the soldiers heard them.

The next day was June 25, the day of the Battle of the Little Big Horn.

Terry knew only that Sioux were gathering in large forces. When Major Marcus A. Reno and his scouting troops found the broad Indian trail, the immediate reaction of the western army was to follow that trail and trap the hostiles as quickly as possible. The reputation of the Indians at that time was that they would run if caught in a pitched battle, and General Terry was not anxious to chase them twice.

Gibbon marched up the Yellowstone River. Custer led his Seventh Cavalry up Rosebud Creek, hot on the Indian trail. When Custer caught sight of the Sioux camp in the distance, he directed Captain McDougall to keep the pack train in the rear while his militia in three sections would do their best to trap the Indians.

Gall was with Sitting Bull when the action started, but he was one of the first to raise the chilling Sioux war whoop and jab his heels to his pony in a chase of the bluecoats. The Hunkpapas were with him, glorying in the chance to do battle.

With Gall's warriors pressing him hard, Reno and his men retreated to the high bluffs. Captain Benteen's troopers joined Reno and his men and they held a quick consultation. Benteen had received a messenger from Custer directing him to send the ammunition and packs forward immediately, and had relayed the order to McDougall who was some distance behind Benteen but coming forward.

They dug in on the bluffs, determined to stick through the night. No one knew where Custer was at the moment. When the first rays of light brightened in the morning, bullets and arrows began zinging toward the soldiers from the Indians again. Gall had returned from his foray against Custer, determined to get Reno.

Toward the middle of the afternoon of that second day the Indians began to withdraw, but the soldiers on the bluffs were kept in their position by constant snipers and sharpshooters. With the wounded bluecoats desperately in need of water, four volunteers slipped to the creek and managed to return with filled canteens.

The dust of Terry's other flank was seen in the distance, and shortly afterwards Sioux quit the attack. From the heights, Reno and Benteen and their men saw the Indians setting fire to the grass in the valley, and then watched as the Sioux nation began to move toward the Big Horn Mountains. The Indians picked up their

Military men in Dakota Territory, probably between 1880-1900. (Photo by W. J. Collins, from the Carper-Tscharner collection)

Enlisted men in camp, 1870's or 1880's. (Photo from the S. Goodale Price collection)

tepees, packed their belongings on the travois and their backs, and with their dogs yelping at their heels began to move the entire fifteen thousand warriors, women, children and equipage to safety in the distant mountains. The battle was over.

Gall told the story of the Little Big Horn himself ten years later, and his story described the fighting personally. He was there. He fought Reno and he fought Custer, he said, and then he fought Reno's soldiers again.

Historians have argued over details of the battle of the Little Big Horn ever since that day when Reno and Benteen and Terry discovered the dead bodies of Custer and the Seventh Cavalry, but Gall says he was there and he helped it happen:

> "We saw the soldiers early in the morning crossing the divide. When Reno and Custer separated, we watched them until they came down into the valley. A cry was raised that the white soldiers were coming, and orders were given for our village to move immediately. Reno swept down so rapidly on the upper end that the Indians were forced to fight.
>
> "Sitting Bull and I were at the point where Reno attacked. Sitting Bull was a big medicine man. The women and children were hastily moved down stream where the Cheyennes were camped. The Sioux attacked Reno, and the Cheyennes Custer, and then all became mixed up.
>
> "The women and children caught the horses for the bucks to mount. Then the bucks mounted and charged back on Reno, checked him and drove him into the timber. The soldiers tied their horses to trees, came out and fought on foot.

"As soon as Reno was beaten and driven back across the river, the whole force turned upon Custer and fought him until they destroyed him. Custer did not reach the river, but was about half a mile up a ravine now called Reno Creek. They fought the soldiers and beat them back, step by step, until all were killed. The Indians ran out of ammunition and then used arrows. They fired from behind their horses. The soldiers got shells stuck in their guns, and had to throw them away. They then fought with little guns (pistols). The Indians were in coulees behind and in front of Custer as he moved up the ridge to take position, and were just as many as the grass.

"The first two companies, Keogh's and Calhoun's, dismounted, and fought on foot. They never broke, but retired, step by step, until forced back to the ridge upon which all finally perished. They were shot down in the line where they stood. Keogh's company rallied by company, and were all killed in a bunch.

"The warriors directed a special fire against the troopers who held the horses while the others fought. As soon as a holder was killed, by waving blankets and great shouting, the horses were stampeded, which made it impossible for the soldiers to escape afterward. The soldiers fought desperately and hard, and never surrendered. They fought standing. They fought in line along the ridge. As fast as the men fell the horses were herded and driven toward the squaws and old men, who gathered them up.

"When Reno attempted to find Custer by throwing out a skirmish line, Custer and all with him were dead. When the skirmishers reached a high point overlooking Custer's field, the Indians were galloping around and over the wounded, dying and dead, popping bullets and arrows into them.

"When Reno made his attack at the upper end he killed my two squaws and three children, which made my heart bad. I then fought with the hatchet (mutilating the soldiers).

"The soldiers ran out of ammunition early in the day. Their supplies of cartridges were in the saddle pockets of their stampeded horses. The Indians then ran up to the soldiers and butchered them with hatchets. A lot of horses ran away and jumped into the river and were caught by the squaws.

"Eleven Indians were killed on Reno Creek, and several Indians fell over and died. Only forty three Indians were killed altogether, but a great many wounded ones came across the river and died in the bushes.

Officers of the Western Army during the Indian wars of the 1870's and 1880's. (Photo from the collection of S. Goodale Price)

Horse bones gathered on Custer's hill before burying them, 1877. (Photo from the Morrow collection, by courtesy of the University of South Dakota Museum)

Some soldiers got away and ran down a ravine, crossed the river, and came back again and were killed.

"We had Oglalas, Minneconjous, Brule, Teton, Uncpapa, Sioux, Cheyenne, Arapahoes and Gros Ventres. When the big dust came in the air down the river (Terry and Gibbon) we struck our lodges and went up a creek toward the White Rain Mountains. The Big Horn ranges were covered with snow. We waited there four days, then went over to the Wyoming mountains." [5]

Other eye witness documents reviewing the fight were made later by several enlisted men.

Gustave Korn, Troop I, United States Cavalry, a troop commanded by Custer, reported at Fort Meade, Dakota Territory on May 21, 1888. Korn says he survived because his horse bolted when Custer gave the command to charge, and Korn could not control him until he was halfway up the bluff when it was too late to return to Custer's men. Korn says Indians were already following Custer into the trap of the ravine, and he thereupon joined Reno's men.

Charles Windolph, Company H under Captain Benteen, Seventh Cavalry, issued a statement in 1940 which he gave to author S. Goodale Price. Windolph told of Benteen's command joining Reno's on the bluff June 25. Both Reno's men and Benteen's dug in for protection during the night, he said, and dawn of June 26 brought additional attack from the Sioux. During the afternoon of June 26 Windolph was one of the men who volunteered to get water for the wounded men. Others with him were Geiger, Meckling and Voit, he said.

Lieutenant W. Scott Edgerly wrote his memory of the battle twice, according to historian Rev. Charles G. DuBois, once at Fort Yates, Dakota Territory which was published in the August 18, 1881 edition of the *Leavenworth Times,* Kansas. The second time he composed a rather long narrative for a lecture which Edgerly gave in 1898. The contents of that lecture was published in the *Rapid City Journal,* 1967, with the notation that it had never been published in written form until that date. Edgerly was a member of D Company, Seventh Cavalry, under the command of Benteen. Edgerly mentions that he and Captain Weir made an effort

Company I troopers decorating Colonel Keogh's grave on Custer's Battlefield, 1877. (Photo from the Morrow collection, by courtesy of the University of South Dakota Museum)

The battlefield map on sign at Garry Owen Historical marker, Wyoming. (Photo by Fielder, 1972)

to find Custer after hearing the heavy firing from Custer's direction, but were forced by Indians to return to Reno.

In any event, when the battle was over Gall fled with Sitting Bull and the other Hunkpapas toward the north country. They managed to get to British Columbia, Canada, safely, and there they stayed while the Black Hills Treaty was signed, while Crazy Horse was killed at Fort Robinson after being persuaded to bring his Oglalas to the Red Cloud Agency in 1877, and while other Sioux tribes were making their peace with the whites.

In Canada there was no peace between Sitting Bull and Gall. Sitting Bull hated the whites for having driven him to exile. Gall may have hated them too, but he realized that he could not spend his life running from the soldiers. The two quarreled. Gall left the northern camp in 1879 with many of the Hunkpapas following him. He was caught in a fight with United States troops in Montana, and lost the battle.

He capitulated to the facts of the day. He would surrender.

In the fall of 1880 he led his people to Poplar River Agency. After discussion of terms, he surrendered to Major Guido Ilges on January 3, 1881. By June 1, 1881, he was in Standing Rock Agency where he pledged cooperation with the United States government with the added promise that he would help run the Standing Rock Agency if requested to do so.

Sitting Bull came to the Standing Rock Agency himself in 1883 after having surrendered July 20, 1881 at Fort Buford. Again the two old friends were living close together, but their friendship had cooled almost to enmity.

The bad feeling between the two was not helped in 1886 when government officials sponsored a ten year commemorative program at Little Big Horn to honor those of the Seventh Cavalry who had died there. Historians, military men, the many others who still remembered that battle came to the Montana hill side. The program chairman asked Gall to speak to the gathering, to tell them what had happened there. He did not ask Sitting Bull, who at the time of the Custer battle had been the general commander of the Indian forces. He asked Gall.

It was then that Gall gave his review of what happened as he remembered it. Kingsbury, in reporting the speech, said:

"Gall is a powerful, fine looking specimen of the red race, forty six years old, and weighs over two hundred pounds. He first appeared reticent, and was inclined to act sullen, but when he stood on the spot which saw the last fight with Custer on earth, his dark eyes lighted with fire, he became earnestly communicative, and told all he knew without restraint. His dignified countenance spoke truthfulness, and there is no doubt that the true history of that dreadful day is at last made known." [6]

Gall was trying to support the Federal Indian policies, and in this he was aided by a strong speaker known as John Grass. Sitting Bull opposed the United States in everything that was proposed to the Hunkpapas. When in 1888 government officials spoke of reducing the size of the Standing Rock lands to set up a permanent Standing Rock Reservation, Gall, Grass and Sitting Bull joined forces and op-

The Reno Monument on the bluffs where Major Reno took his stand in the Custer Battlefield. (Photo by Fielder, 1972)

The Mass Monument at Custer Battlefield. (Photo by Fielder, 1972)

The steamer *Far West* taking cargo. The *Far West* was the steamship which carried Reno's wounded from the Battle of the Little Big Horn back to civilization after the death of Custer and his Seventh Cavalry in 1876. (Photo from the Morrow collection, by courtesy of the University of South Dakota Museum)

posed the movement. The three chiefs were brought to Washington, but they managed to deadlock the proposal for nearly a year. Finally in 1889 Gall could see that they were getting nowhere, and that the Washington officials were in a position to take everything from the Indians if the Hunkpapas would not talk their kind of sense, so he signed the land transfer.

As a result of his capitulation Gall gained the complete enmity of Sitting Bull, but in contrast he was made a judge of the Court of Indian Offenses at Standing Rock by the Commissioner of Indian Affairs.

Records say Gall was a good judge. He meant what he pledged when he said he would cooperate with the white people. Even the wild Messiah belief that swept the Sioux nation and the Indians as far as the west coast did not affect Gall's loyalty to the government once he had made up his mind to support the Great White Father. He heard that Sitting Bull was encouraging the ghost shirt dancing of the Messiah religion, and Gall issued a statement against ghost shirt dancing. There was no more friendship between the two men.

Sitting Bull was killed in 1890 when he resisted arrest during the Messiah uprising. The massacre of Sioux at Wounded Knee that followed shortly thereafter was a time of mourning for all the Sioux wherever they might be, but Gall was not at Wounded Knee.

Ford at the Little Big Horn River where Reno first crossed prior to the battle at the Custer Battlefield. (Photo by Fielder, 1972)

People walking along the bluffs where Reno and his men fought at the Custer Battlefield. (Photo by Fielder, 1972)

Garry Owen Historical marker, where Reno was turned back by the Indians toward the retreat to the bluffs. (Photo by Fielder, 1972)

The museum at the Custer Battlefield, near the Mass Monument. (Photo by Fielder, 1972)

The white stone showing where General Custer's body was found is shown at approximately center of cluster of stones near the Mass Monument. Each square white tombstone marks the spot where one of the dead bodies were found. (Photo by Fielder 1972)

Indian lecturers at the museum, Custer Battlefield. One is dressed in a cavalry uniform of the 1870's, the other in a "Plains Indian" costume typical of several Sioux tribes of the 1870's. (Photo by Fielder, 1972)

He stayed at Standing Rock Reservation, acting as a judge whenever called upon to do so, working as a farmer between court sessions.

In 1894 he died at the age of 56, a big man physically, a powerful leader, a man with memories of fighting for what he believed to be right. For many years he had believed that fighting was the only option he had—until a day when he decided there was another way to help his people.

That he could completely reverse himself for the sake of his followers is a mark of the man's greatness. Gall was one of the mightiest of Sioux warrior chiefs.

One of the mightiest.

Quoted References: Gall, Reno's Opponent.

[1] "Gall's Oratory Impressed Country," *Rapid City Daily Journal*, Rapid City, South Dakota.

[2] "Gall's Oratory," opus cited.

[3] "Gall's Oratory," opus cited.

[4] "Gall's Oratory," opus cited.

[5] Kingsbury, George W., *History of Dakota Territory*. The S. J. Clarke Publishing Company, 1915. Chicago, Illinois. p. 967.

[6] Kingsbury, opus cited, p. 967.

5

MARTIN CHARGER AND THE SHETAK CAPTIVES

One Feather's brother was dead, killed by the Crow Indians, and One Feather was giving a feast in his memory. The Sans Arc tribe sat in small groups around the campfire, eating buffalo meat and helping One Feather in his sorrow.

Ten year old Charger, known by the Indian name Wowacinye meaning Dependable, watched with wide eyes. One Feather went from warrior to warrior as they ate, and he laid his hands on the head of each.

"I swear," said One Feather, "by the warriors in all the Sans Arc tribe, you who are my friends, that I will get revenge on the Crows for this killing."

Dependable saw, and heard, and in his heart he decided that some day he would grow up to be a great warrior. He was greatly surprised when the feast was over and the day was past, and another day was past, and his father Turkey Head summoned Dependable and his brother Little Hawk into his tipi.

Turkey Head said, "Sit, my sons."

They sat obediently, waiting.

Turkey Head said, his voice solemn, "I have known the customs of the Indians all my life, and there are some things we do that are not good. The life of an Indian is full of pride. There are acts in a war party which give an Indian honor—striking the enemy with a lance, to be wounded, to steal the ponies of the enemy. But these are not all, my sons."

What could be better, young Dependable wondered, and his father answered the unspoken question.

"Generosity to your fellow tribesmen," said Turkey Head, "is far more important than fighting."

Dependable sat straight, shocked at the words.

"If you cannot offer food to your brothers and friends," Turkey Head emphasized to his sons, "you are of no account. Even if you are a great warrior, if you are not generous to your friends, you are nothing."

It was a thought that Dependable had not entertained before. Again, he was very impressed.

His boyhood name was changed to Wa-ana-tan, The Charger, and many years later he added the white name of Martin so he was known as Martin Charger. He was born in 1833 between the present towns of Sturgis and Rapid City in the valley called the race track which surrounds the Black Hills. Turkey Head, his father, was the son of a white man named Lewis, but there have been conflicting claims whether he was the son of Meriwether Lewis of Lewis and Clark expedition fame, or whether he was the son Reuben Lewis, a fur trader from St. Louis. Martin's son Samuel Charger and Dr. Charles E. Deland, South Dakota historian, say Turkey Head was the son of Meriwether Lewis. Doane Robinson, South Dakota historian, and Louis LaPlant, trader married to an Indian wife, both claim that Reuben Lewis was his father. In any case, Turkey Head was half white, half Indian.

Martin's mother was a Sans Arc Indian named Her Good Road. Turkey Head was employed by the American Fur Company as a trader, and as such traded with the Rees (Aricara) and Mandans.

The boy Dependable became The Charger, and though he pondered his father's words as he grew older, the excitement of war parties remained to tantalize him. When he was eighteen, nearly a grown man, he and Little Hawk joined the warrior uncles of his mother's family in a war party against the Crows.

Martin Charger. (Photo
by permission of South
Dakota Historical Society)

Victorious, the Sioux returned bearing proud news of Charger's ability on the battlefield. He was invited to join the Grass Society because of his bravery.

The next year when he was nineteen, Martin Charger married a Yankton Sioux girl, Walking Hail, in the year when the 1851 treaty was signed at Fort Laramie. He was a man with the responsibility of a family. He remembered his father's advice. He had proven his ability as a fighter, and he could choose the other way if he wanted it. With Walking Hail helping with the food, Charger began to give feasts to his friends, to visiting tribes, even to his enemies. He was the first Sans Arc to invite their traditional enemies, the Crows, to join in a feast. The Crows came, and Charger gave them horses besides food.

As he noted the results of the friendship which he offered, Martin Charger became convinced that his father had been right. When war parties were organized against the Rees Charger did not go. He might have given up fighting entirely, but it was all around him. General William S. Harney, called the Hornet by the Indians, attacked Chief Little Thunder and then made his headquarters at Fort Pierre on the Missouri River.

Charger did not fight. He spent all his time organizing parties to reach the hostile bands of Aricara and the Crows, urging them to come to Fort Pierre for negotiation with General Harney. In the spring of 1856 they came. Charger gave feasts to all, talking to them when they came, urging them to know peace between themselves and with the whites. One man could not change them so quickly. When the treaty council ended the Sioux and Crow Indians battled again, as always. In 1860 Chief Big Crow was killed, and in 1861 Crow Feather, chief of the Sans Arc, met death in battle.

Charger led the peaceful tribes gathered around Fort Pierre, trying to influence those who came to the fort for trading. Sometimes they listened, other times they did not.

In the year 1860 a friend of Charger's named Kills-Game-and-Comes-Back had a remarkable dream which he told to Charger. Kills Game and Comes Back saw ten black stags, he said, and the leading stag said to him, "This vision is to be fulfilled by you and to be complied with by all who are members. You and every member is to be respected and feared and you must be united in your undertakings." [1]

Charger and Kills Game and Comes Back asked several of their friends to join in a council with them to try to interpret the dream. They could not agree, and held another council. Their friends Swift Bird and Four Bears were there. The suggestion was made that the vision meant a group of ten braves who should combine for the good of the tribe, being generous with food and property. Kills Game urged a clause naming revenge against enemies within their tribe, but Charger disagreed.

Again they counciled, inviting Charging Dog, a medicine man, to join them. They smoked a pipe of peace, considering the vision.

Finally Charging Dog said, "We may be brave in battle, but as everybody knows we do not live long and to do each other harm in our camp is very bad. I have seen a lot of it during my life. I believe the hardest thing for anybody to do is to do good to others, but it makes their hearts rejoice." [2]

So the young men organized a group of five good braves to start the thing, and called themselves the Fool Soldiers. The name was just a name, as other groups in the Sioux tribes were called Artichoke Eaters, or Broken Bow band. In fact it was the Artichoke Eaters of the hostile Hunkpapas who threatened to kill Chief Bear Ribs when they came to Fort Pierre.

Though the Fool Soldiers, headed by Charger and Kills Game, took Chief Bear Ribs into their tipi at the fort to protect him, he was enticed by someone to come outside for a talk. Bear Ribs went to talk with the caller, and was shot by the traitor before the Fool Soldiers could rescue him.

There was a great deal of excitement after the killing. The lower Yanktonai band came from the east side of the river. The main group of Sioux, including Charger's Sans Arc tribe, went riding toward the fort with all haste. The Hunkpapas moved quickly toward Fort Pierre, not wanting to miss the fighting.

It could have been a riot, but Charger and his Fool Soldier band stood quickly and called the angry Indians around them. Charger suggested a feast. Catching the interest of the several tribes, he immediately assigned portions of the preparation to different ones. The feast was made, and when they were ready to eat Charger talked to them again.

"It is a disgrace to fight among ourselves," he said. "We are all related. We have many of the same ancestors. I call the son of Chief Bear Ribs forward, so I may give him a horse in his sorrow."

The feast and talk worked. The Hunkpapas agreed that they would not fight. The next day the killing was forgotten and the different tribes began trading at the fort in peace.

The success of Charger's mission gave him considerable prestige among the Sioux tribes as a peace maker. When they returned to Fort Pierre in 1862 after a winter camp in the Black Hills country, they heard of an attack by the Santee Sioux against the white settlers in Minnesota and Dakota Territory. Colonel John Pattee, commander of troops in the Dakota country, wrote to his superiors in reporting the affair:

"about the last of August, 1862 . . . we received the news of the most terrible massacre that ever occurred in the United States. The Yellow Medicine Indian Agency was captured by Santee Indians in

Drawing of Bird's Eye View of the Black Hills, from the Jenney-Newton survey, 1875, showing their conception of the red soil "race-track" encircling the Black Hills of South Dakota.
  Martin Charger was born in 1833 on this race track.

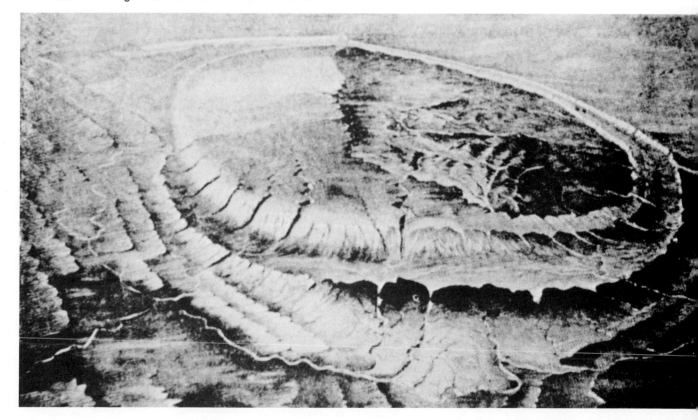

First and Second chiefs of the Mandans. Martin Charger's father, Turkey Head, traded with the Mandans as an employee of the American Fur Company when Martin was only a boy. (Photo from Kingsbury, "History of Dakota Territory," 1915)

Minnesota. Five counties were depopulated and 800 white people were massacred in the most revolting and cruel manner. A number of women and children were made prisoners by the Indians . . . " [3]

All Indians other than the hostile Santees were ordered to move to the west side of the Missouri River. Chief Angry Eyes, Two Kettle band of Sioux, was killed in a misunderstanding between the Two Kettle band and the white soldiers, which only added to the seriousness of the total situation.

Charger and the Fool Soldiers tried to advocate neutrality among the tribes.

"Let the white soldiers take care of the Santees," he advised. "We will remain peaceful."

Councils were held. Chief Tall Mandan of the Two Kettle band called for revenge for the death of Chief Angry Eyes. In the general distrust, word came down river that the hostile Santees under Chief White Lodge were holding some white captives.

During those years of the early 1860's boats plied the Missouri and Yellowstone rivers, carrying miners from the Idaho gold strikes, military men, adventurers and others. Charles Galpin and a party of miners were moving down the river in November 1862 and were stopped by the hostile Santees. Galpin stopped, but managed to persuade the Santees to release him. As he was getting ready to push from the bank, one of the captive white women appeared on the

76

river bank and pleaded to be rescued. He learned from her that Mrs. Wright and Mrs. Duly with six children were prisoners of the Santee Sioux camped nearby.

Galpin could do nothing alone, so he and his crew continued down the river. Fort Pierre, a hundred miles distant, was the first stopping place although the nearest troops were farther downstream at Fort Randall. Fort LaFramboise was only three miles northwest of Fort Pierre. Galpin reached Fort Pierre November 17, 1862, and told his story to Charles Primeau, superior commandant in charge.

Martin Charger and Kills Game and Comes Back with the rest of the Fool Soldier band were there when Galpin reported the story.

The Fool Soldiers numbered the full quota of ten by that time: Charger, Kills Game and Comes Back, Four Bears, Mad Bear, Pretty Bear, One Rib, Strikes Fire, Red Dog, Charging Dog, and Swift Bird. That night they held a secret meeting. According to an account written later by Martin Charger's son Samuel:

Four Bears, Two Kettle tribe of the Dakota Sioux. Four Bears was one of the ten members of the Fool-Soldier band which rescued the Shetak captives in 1862. He became a prominent member of his tribe, his name being one of the signers of the 1876 treaty for the cession of the Black Hills. (Photo by B. H. Gurnsey, probably 1870, by courtesy of the Smithsonian Institution National Anthropological Archives)

"Charger advocated the organization should unite in their convictions and all the captives should be liberated at all costs, thus putting into practice all that their organization stood for. With the danger confronting their Sioux tribe and their faith in Charger to find a way out of the situation, the Indians agreed to take Charger's advice." [4]

With Martin Charger and Kills Game and Comes Back leading them, the young Indians approached Charles Primeau and bought coffee and sugar, paying Primeau in furs. The negotiable material tucked safely in bags on their horses, they rode up river to find the Santees and the eight captives, hoping to trade with the Santees for the prisoners.

It was a crazy thing to do in view of the existing hard feelings between red and white men, nevertheless the Fool Soldiers met the Santees opposite the mouth of the Grand River. They took a day to parley and trade, but on Novembver 20, one day after they reached camp, they had the captives in their possession and started down stream.

They arrived at Fort LaFramboise, then continued to Fort Pierre on November 24, where Primeau gave them

"calico, cotton cloth and red flannel with which they clothed themselves quite comfortably." [5]

Galpin had reached Fort Randall on the 19th with his story of the captives, and Colonel Pattee arrived there the 21st. Hearing of the situation, Colonel Pattee immediately began making preparations to take troops up the river to effect a rescue, and started to move on the 26th. Pattee was entirely too late. On November 29 Pattee and his troops met the freed women and children traveling by wagon down the river trail about two miles north of Ponca Creek, with Frederick Dupree and Louis LaPlant. He was able to give an explicit account of their trials.

The women and children had come from the Lake Shetak area in Minnesota, he says, and subsequently were called the Shetak captives. They included Mrs. Duly and two daughters, the oldest about twelve years old; Mrs. Julia Wright and her five year old son; Lillie Everett, about six years old, whose mother had been killed at the time of the massacre; and two girls by the name of Ireland. While held by the Santees, the women had been treated with utter contempt, traded by the Indian men for their pleasure, kicked and abused by the Indian women. They were made to do the menial work around the camp, tending fires, carrying wood and water, putting up Indian lodges. Their clothing had been taken from them and they were wearing rags and discarded Indian moccasins when rescued.

Pattee and his men cooked for them, provided a tent, a Sibley stove and blankets, and took up a collection of money. He was instrumental in sending a letter to a Sioux City paper and a Cedar Falls paper listing their names and ages to notify relatives or friends who could help them, and then sent them with an escort back to Fort Randall to be quartered with his wife there until they could be conducted back to civilization.

As soon as the Shetak captives reached Fort Randall and the haven of Colonel Pattee's home, Mrs. Duly promptly went to bed and

"was not able to sit up for fifteen days," [6]

but rest and food improved the health of all and they were able to travel again twenty nine days later. Brigadier General John Cook came to get the group

The Sioux were still following their ancient culture of burying their dead on posts above the prairie lands, when Martin Charger was a young man. (Photo from Kingsbury, "History of Dakota Territory," 1915)

toward the end of December and took them down the river to Yankton Agency in Dakota Territory, then to Sioux City, Iowa. Mrs. Wright's husband met them at Yankton Agency. Lillie Everett's father appeared at Sioux City to claim the little girl. The others continued to Fort Dodge, Iowa, before Mr. Duly arrived to greet his wife. The men had supposed their families were killed during the massacre, until alerted by the newspaper notices of their rescue and safety.

Mrs. Duly's health and spirit had been broken completely by her sojourn with the Indians. Three weeks after she rejoined her husband she lost her sanity

"and became a harmless imbecile," [7]

according to Colonel Pattee's report. Little Lillie Everett grew up and married W. R. Brown of New York City, but the others dropped out of sight.

Pattee claims that, having assured himself of the safety of the group, he made a full report to the United States government and urged that a liberal allowance be made to the Fool Soldiers for their part in rescuing the white captives. He said:

79

Fort Pierre, Dakota Territory, 1832, on the Missouri River. Though the rescue of the Shetak captives occurred in 1862, some thirty years later than this photo, the old fort was much the same at that time. (Photo from Kingsbury, *History of Dakota Territory*)

"I had been informed that the United States congress had appropriated $2400 to pay those Indians for their trouble and was greatly pleased that the government had recognized the obligation." [8]

On the other hand, five of the Fool Soldiers band later swore to Doane Robinson, South Dakota historian, that they had never had a cent paid them in any way. They had rescued the women and children on their own initiative and paid with their own peltries for the coffee and sugar which they used as trade to the Santee for their release.

From the Indians' viewpoint, it was certainly a dangerous thing to do. Martin Charger and his friends were not only part of the great Sioux nation, as were the Santee Sioux who held the prisoners, they were a part of the great Sioux nation actively engaged in harassing the whites as a general policy. They had committed an act that could not be forgotten, though it took a long time before the whites publicly gave them any credit.

Charger knew this would be his life work regardless of what came next. The next year he went north to visit his uncle One Ghost, and told him of the Shetak captives and their rescue. One Ghost immediately supported Charger's actions, and returned with his nephew to the Sans Arc band.

Charger was in various places during the next year, Fort Randall, on the Bad River in the Slim Butte country, in the Black Hills country again for hunting. Charger and part of his Sans Arc band camped briefly near Fort Sully. When they heard of Sioux on Medicine Creek who were starving, the Fool Soldiers traded robes for food at the fort and took the food to their starving friends. Finding the group destitute, the Fool Soldiers stayed to care for them through the winter, then escorted them to Fort Pierre to camp.

In 1867 Martin Charger's good friend Kills Game and Comes Back was killed by a Santee, Gray Face, as a revenge for the rescue of the Shetak captives. Kills Game was brought to Fort Rice and buried nearby. An old tradition in some Indian tribes was that when one of two close friends dies, the other also must die. For a while Charger was guarded lest he commit suicide, but Martin knew that it was more important that he live in spite of his grief for his friend.

It was the next year, 1868, when Charger was asked to be one of the Indian delegates to Washington, D. C. to discuss the boundaries of the proposed great Sioux Reservation which would be offered in Fort Laramie that year. He went to Washington. This was important and he knew it, but he did not go to Fort Laramie for the treaty council. His friends advised him to stay away. There would be Santee Indians at the treaty council, and the Sioux nation knew that Charger was the man behind the Shetak rescue.

Charger and his Fool Soldiers camped near the Fort Bennett Agency, from where they continued to operate in their program of peace. When in 1869 a hostile band stole horses from friends of the Sans Arc, Charger went to search for the stolen horses. With his uncles helping him he found the horses and returned them to their owners. While he was doing that, his own Sans Arc people went to war against the Crows. Fifteen Sans Arc were slain. Charger moved among the sorrowing Sans Arc, trying to convince them that they must move back to the reservation which the 1868 Fort Laramie Treaty had assigned to them. Gradually he was convincing them.

The Sans Arc were still living on the buffalo of the land for their main sustenance, and the buffalo were disappearing from the land. Terrific slaughter of the beasts by government hunters caused the numbers of buffalo to decrease more every year, and as the buffalo died the Sioux could see their meat, their hides, their whole buffalo economy disappearing.

Charger could see a complete change of their way of living. In 1872 he led his friends to a camp across the river from Fort Bennett, and there started building log

"The Rescue of the Shetak Captives," mural in the Mobridge auditorium, Mobridge, South Dakota, painted by Oscar Howe. The two wheeled cart shown is known as a Red River Cart, the women and children being conducted by their Indian rescuers to Fort Pierre in 1862. (Photo from *Aberdeen American-News*, Aberdeen, South Dakota)

Louis LaPlant, one of the white traders who helped in the rescue of the Shetak captives after the Fool Soldiers had recovered them from the Santees. (Photo by courtesy of Adams Memorial Hall, Deadwood, South Dakota)

houses with chimneys. The reservation agents had been encouraging the farming of lands by the Indians, and Charger decided to give farming a try. Other Indians began to join him, raising corn and vegetables. It was the first Indian community in the country.

When Charger was summoned with others to Washington to discuss negotiations for the cession of the Black Hills to white entry, he went willingly. Charger insisted that only a three fourths majority of Indian approval would be adequate for selling the Black Hills, and a treaty council to secure the majority vote was arranged between the Red Cloud and Spotted Tail Agencies in 1875. A report was made, but the treaty was still pending when General George A. Custer was ordered to launch a campaign against the hostile northern Sioux. Samuel Charger insists his father called a meeeting of Indian head men and chiefs to meet with Custer. A feast was made, and the Indians held a council with Custer, but the project was hopeless. In June, Charger and the Fool Soldiers heard that Custer and his Seventh Cavalry had been killed in the Battle of the Little Big Horn.

Custer dead, the military men began the task of bringing all hostiles to Indian agencies. The Black Hills Treaty council was reopened, and this time the Black Hills Treaty was signed on October 27, 1876. The name Wa-an-atan (The Charger) was on that treaty with nine other chiefs from the Sans Arc tribe. His co-worker in the Fool Soldiers group, Four Bears, signed under the name Ma-to-to-pa for the Two Kettle tribe.

After the signing, Charger and his band moved to the west side of the Missouri River and camped opposite Little Bend. Black Feet and Two Kettle Indians joined the Sans Arc community there. In 1878 cows were issued to the peaceful Indians, but they needed the range land for the cows' forage. Chief Swan, Minneconjou, was assigned the Cheyenne River and Cherry Creek area. Charger took his people to the Cheyenne River where the Cheyenne Agency was located in 1880.

Martin encouraged the building of log houses, the herding of the stock, the cutting of hay for winter feed. He accepted the white man's mowing machine and taught his people how to use it. They cut wood and corded it to sell to steamboats on the river. They raised wheat, and corn which they ground into corn meal at nearby Forest City. Through all the growing enterprise of the Cheyenne Agency

Indians, Charger was considered their leader. Through his influence with Bishop Hare his community was granted a church building, though the Indians were still worshipping medicine men more than the Christian religion. Charger was not discouraged. He sent one of his sons-in-law, John Promise, to a Yankton Agency Mission School and then welcomed him home as a missionary worker.

In 1887 Charger was recalled to Washington, D. C. with other Sioux chiefs to discuss the Allotment Act, or the Dawes Act. The treaty of 1889 opened all the country between the Cheyenne River and the White River, the Indians to get an allotment of 640 acres for each family head, with persons of 18 years or over to receive 320 acres. Minor children drew 160 acres each. Farm implements, stock were part of the agreement.

It seemed that Martin Charger's dream of peace with the white government was actually becoming a reality, when the 1890 Messiah Craze erupted in Indian lands. The medicine men relayed the message everywhere:

> "a new world was coming for the Indian which would cover the old world, and when it came the dead would come to life." [9]

The buffalo would come back. All would be as it was before the white men came to the western prairies.

A dream, certainly, but a dream that caught the imaginations of the Sioux and all Indians in the west. Charger did not believe it. He tried to tell his people that it was a mistake. He made feasts, which had been successful before, but the ghost dancing continued. In spite of all he could do, the people of the Sans Arc heard of the killing of Sitting Bull on the Standing Rock Reservation, the killing of Big Foot and his camp at Wounded Knee, and the crying and wailing of the Indians when the dead were counted.

Martin Charger and the missionary workers of his community went to meet the survivors of Big Foot's band and brought them to the reservation. Charger

Colonel John Pattee's home and school house at Cherokee, North Carolina, 1896. John Pattee and family stand in front of the house.

Colonel Pattee started to move toward the rescue of the Shetak captives on November 26, but met them in the hands of their Indian rescuers November 29. Pattee and his men assumed their protection at that time, sent letters to newspapers to find relatives and quartered them with his wife at Fort Randall until they could be rested and sent down stream to civilization. (Photo by "C. M. F.," 1896, by courtesy of the Smithsonian Institution National Anthropological Archives)

Steamboat landing at Yankton, Dakota Territory, 1878. The rescued captives were taken by Brigadier General John Cook down river to Yankton Agency in December 1862. Mrs. Wright's husband met her at the Yankton Agency, but the others continued further down river. (Photo from the Morrow collection, by courtesy of the University of South Dakota Museum)

talked to them, reminding them of the history of the Indian, telling them their only salvation was the teaching of Christianity. They must learn to live at peace with the whites, he said; and they listened.

Following the Indian custom, Martin Charger had two wives at the time, Walking Hail and Wasumaniwin, or Eliza. To set an example for the others, Martin married Eliza in the Christian church to comply with the laws of the state. If he did so, he knew that his followers would do the same. The reason for having more than one wife had always been the need for more hands to do the work of the camp, especially when the man of the house was the generous chief who gave many feasts. If the white man's law said one wife must be married legally, and only one, Martin Charger did so.

In recognition of his continued services, the United States government built Martin a frame house about a mile west of the Cheyenne River Agency in 1887. He helped to select a new location for the Cheyenne Agency site in 1890, and moved with it to the new location the next year. He became a Judge of the Indian Court, always working for the benefit and welfare of his tribe. When some of his Indian police force killed a white man named Field in 1892, Charger employed legal counsel for the Indian defendants. That year, in 1892, he went again to Washington to discuss allotments for the Indians on the Bad River. Whenever they needed him, however they needed him, Martin Charger was strongly instrumental in leading his people to lasting friendship with the whites.

The last convention he attended was at Yankton Agency in 1899.

He became ill in his home the morning of August 16, 1900, and died that afternoon. Friends and relatives from various Sioux reservations came to pay their last respects. He was buried in the cemetery near the first Cheyenne Agency location which he had helped to select in 1880. His family and friends recognized his great

84

The Sioux delegation to Washington, D. C., May-June 1875, called there for discussion of the Black Hills cession. The Indian seated at front, fifth from the left, is believed to be Martin Charger. His friend, Four Bears, signed the 1876 treaty for the Black Hills with Charger, and could be the second from left in the front row. (Photo by courtesy of the Smithsonian Institution National Anthropological Archives)

Cheyenne Warrors in Council. Martin Charger helped to select a new location for the Cheyenne Agency in 1890, and was a Judge of the Indian Court at the agency. He led many an Indian council while there, always trying to lead his people to friendship with the whites. (Photo from Kingsbury, ''History of Dakota Territory,'' 1915)

Samuel Charger (son of Martin Charger), left; and a friend, Luke Gilbert. (Photo by courtesy of the South Dakota Historical Society)

influence with the tombstone inscription: "A generous and wise Chief, a friend of the white people." [10]

Forty seven years after the rescue of the Shetak captives by the Fool Soldiers, the South Dakota Historical Society erected a granite monument in 1909 upon the site where the Shetak captives were rescued by the Indian men. On the stone were chiseled the words: "Shetak Captives Rescued Here November 1862 by Fool Soldiers Band." The Old Settlers' Association of Walworth county provided a suitable base, dedicating it June 16, 1909. The story might have ended there except for the fact that the monument began to move—not of its own volition, of course, but it would not stay in one place.

Shortly after the dedication, Mobridge constructed a park near the center of town and the monument was moved there. Later, the town fathers developed Riverside Park two miles west of town, and the migratory marker was moved to Riverside Park about a mile and a half from the actual scene of the rescue. It remained there until the waters of Oahe Dam on the Missouri River began backing over the lands below Mobridge. The site of the Indian camp where the

knowing they had only the possibility of derision or hostility as reward. No man can do better than that.

In 1929 the federal government erected a monument for famous chiefs of the Cheyenne River Reservation. Martin Charger's name was on the list. South Dakota's senator Peter Norbeck was one of the main speakers at the service, and many notable persons attended the dedication of the monument.

Martin left two sons, Samuel Charger and Harry Charger. Samuel married Rosa Red Weasel at LaPlant, South Dakota, and had a son Philip E. Charger born October 27, 1909. Samuel carried on his father's tradition by acting as Tribal Council Chairman, Government employee, County Constable, Justice of the Peace, Field Representative for the law firm of Case & Calhoun for 21 years, and took an active part in matters affecting his people all his life.Harry Charger was educated in Philadelphia at a non-reservation school.

His two daughters were Sophie Left Handed Bear and Jane Grey Bear, but we have no information on their life after their father's death.

Martin Charger was one of the first who accepted the white civilization whole heartedly. He recognized the value of friendship rather than warfare, and worked for peace in a day when there was little peace between red and white men. It can be said now that he achieved that peace in the communities which his life touched.

One man can do little? It is not so. When the man is Martin Charger, one man can do much.

Quoted References: Martin Charger, and the Shetak Captives.

[1] Charger, Samuel, "Biography of Martin Charger," *South Dakota History Collections,* Vol. XXII, 1946. p. 5.

[2] Charger, Samuel, opus cited, p. 6.

[3] Pattee, John, "Reminiscences of John Pattee," edited by Doane Robinson, *South Dakota History Collections,* Vol. V, 1910, pp. 282-283.

[4] Charger, Samuel, opus cited, p. 11.

[5] Pattee, John, opus cited, p. 286.

[6] Pattee, John, opus cited, p. 289.

[7] Pattee, John, opus cited, p. 289.

[8] Pattee, John, opus cited, p. 286.

[9] Charger, Samuel, Opus cited, p. 21.

[10] Charger, Samuel, opus cited, p. 25.

RED CLOUD, THE SCHEMER

Feuding had always existed between Sioux tribes and other Indians of the prairie country. The Sioux were a tremendous, roaming conglomerate mixture of various inner tribes. When their enemies attacked them the Sioux joined as brothers to each other, but there were times when the Sioux fought each other. Thus it was in 1841.

In the Oglala Sioux camp many were angered at some disagreement. The Oglala and Brules lived north of the Platte River, the Cheyennes and Arapahoes were south in the Republican River country. Former friends and allies, the two groups fought hard. As anger spread over the valleys of the rolling prairie, suddenly a young man with a scarlet blanket over his shoulders led a battalion of friends sporting similar red blankets, and the group covered the hillside.

"Like a red cloud," said one of the Oglalas, pointing to the rushing horses. The crimson horde swept forward. Seeing themselves overpowered, the enemy turned and fled.

Afterwards, when they were recounting the day's battle, the men thought of the simile again. They pointed toward the young warrior, and chief Man Afraid of His Horses said, "You shall be known as Red Cloud to remember this day."

Red Cloud, Mahkpia-luta, smiled with pride. Only nineteen years old, he had proved his worth as a warrior. He had been born near the site of North Platte, Nebraska in 1822, when only buffalo moved there in the prairie wind and no white man knew the camp.

The Oglala Sioux had known Man Afraid's family as chieftains for many generations, but Man Afraid of His Horses had a son and the boy was still a child at the time. The name was sometimes translated to mean Man of Whose Horses They are Afraid, and sometimes just called Man Afraid, but the name was a proud one. The chief was a fearless fighter and a strong leader of men, but he was growing older and his son was not ready to take the hereditary chieftainship.

After Red Cloud had shown his bravery, Man Afraid often asked him to fight by his side as his trusted lieutenant. Gradually through the years, Man Afraid advanced Red Cloud to head soldier and then to war chief. He could not give him the chieftainship because that heritage belonged to his son, Young Man Afraid of His Horses, but in the meantime Red Cloud led the Oglala warriors.

In 1851 a treaty was held at Fort Laramie in which various Sioux and other northwest tribes, the Assiniboines, Arikaras, the Gros Ventres, Crows, Cheyennes and Arapahoes promised peace between themselves, even naming one great chief among them, Conquering Bear, to be mediator of all. The treaty was tentatively a good thought, but too good to last. For the next three years the prairies were comparatively peaceful. The incident that ruined the peace was known afterwards as the Grattan massacre.

On August 17, 1854, some Mormon emigrants passed the Sioux camp of Conquering Bear near Fort Laramie, including Oglala, Brules and Wahzazhe Sioux. A cow wandered from the Mormon camp and into the Indian camp. Though the cow was said to be tough and sinewy, the Indians shot it with some glee (it was trespassing, there is no doubt) and ate the animal.

The Mormon demanded his cow, but the cow was dead and gone. To facilitate justice, the Commandant at Fort Laramie sent Lieutenant John Grattan with 29 men and an interpreter to arrest the Indian who killed the cow. The cow killer happened to be a Minneconjou Indian named High Forehead who was visiting

Red Cloud in Sioux head-dress. (Photo by Graves Studio, from *Rapid City Holiday Greetings*, 1919-1920)

the Sioux, and Conquering Bear (also called The Bear or Brave Bear) refused to give him to authorities for arrest.

Lieutenant Grattan ordered his men to fire. In the melee which followed, Conquering Bear was killed, he who had been named as chief head man of the Sioux tribes at the 1851 treaty. Infuriated, the Sioux fell on Grattan's men and killed every one. They rushed to the trading house of James Bordeaux and took what they wanted, then stole the annuity goods ordered by P. Choteau. They were avenged, but Conquering Bear was killed and Lieutenant Grattan and his men were just as dead.

Fetterman Monument, Wyoming, marks the spot where Red Cloud and his warriors killed eighty men in an effort to force the abandonment of the Bozeman Trail in 1866. (Photo by Fielder, 1971)

Red Cloud wearing the black suit which he preferred for his visits to Washington. (Photo from Doane Robinson, *History of South Dakota*)

Peace on the prairies was ended.

The Sioux laughed at the 1851 treaty of friendship. They would harass the whites on the Oregon Trail whenever they had the opportunity. They would fight with each other if they wanted.

In some kind of effort to control the ravaging Sioux, General William S. Harney led a foray against the Indians in 1855 on the Bluewater, and there he reversed the situation. It was Harney who attacked, Harney who killed the Indian village, and the Sioux who took the beating. Though the Bluewater battle was against the Brule Sioux, it touched deeply in the hearts of the Oglala as well. Red Cloud may not have been at Bluewater, indeed there is no indication that he was—but the Sioux brothers were Sioux brothers, and General Harney, the Hornet, had taken the gauntlet with vengence.

Red Cloud determined to fight back in every way that he could.

When the Sioux fought their ancient enemies, the Crows, sometime in the 1860's, Red Cloud led them. Man Afraid was no longer in the forefront of the fighting. Young Man Afraid was made a Shirt Wearer in the traditional ceremony of picking promising young Oglala men for future chieftainships. Others chosen with him in the ceremony were young Crazy Horse, American Horse, and Sword, all young men of brilliant promise. Red Cloud watched from the sidelines. He knew that he, Red Cloud, was the Oglala warrior who fought the fights of the Sioux, whom the braves would follow into battle. These young men, the new Shirt Wearers, still had to prove themselves before they could become chiefs.

When news came in 1863 that the government was opening a road to Montana along the Powder River, long a good hunting ground of the Sioux, Red Cloud rebelled.

92

Red Cloud and his wife. Some historians say that Red Cloud had only one wife, contrary to Indian custom at that time, but only because his wife refused to allow another woman in her tepee. (Photo by Heyn & Matzen, date not recorded, copyright ca. 1900. By courtesy of Smithsonian Institution, National Anthropological Archives)

Indian peace commissioners at Fort Laramie. This photograph is apparently undated, but several peace councils were held at Fort Laramie. This may have been the 1868 council which was held to terminate the harassment against the Bozeman Trail forts, and to designate the large Sioux reservation in the western half of present South Dakota. Red Cloud signed, but not until three forts had been officially abandoned by the military. (Photo by courtesy of National Archives)

He stood straight and tall by the Sioux camp, and his words rang in the night air, "I will kill any white who comes into Indian country!"

Shouts of approval greeted his words. From that time, he took every opportunity to engage the white soldiers in the hit-and-run battle tactics of the Indians, and he knew he was hurting.

When the Sioux were invited to a treaty council at Fort Laramie in 1866, Red Cloud refused to sign the proffered treaty. The two years following have been called the Red Cloud War, and well they might be. His first big victory was at Fort Phil Kearny along the Bozeman Trail in Wyoming. On December 21, 1866 he gathered his warriors around the fort and planned his attack. He had two thousand men with him, eager for battle. Crazy Horse and several others were sent from the main body of Sioux fighters to coax the soldiers from the fort by stampeding some government horses. Colonel Carrington, Commandant, sent Captain William Judd Fetterman to disperse the raiders. Fetterman rode hard after Crazy Horse's decoys and straight into the trap laid by the wily Red Cloud. Eighty men died, but Red Cloud lived to fight again.

He asked Spotted Tail, chief of the Brules, to join him, but Spotted Tail elected to live in peace with the white men. Red Cloud snorted his derision. He would fight without Spotted Tail.

In the summer of 1867 he continued his war in earnest. Dividing his men in two forces, he attacked Fort C. F. Smith on July 31 and August 1 at the Wagon Box Fight, and Fort Phil Kearny the next day. The army was prepared with better rifles and with the knowledge that they had an angry man waiting to attack. The Sioux suffered heavy losses at both battles, and Red Cloud was forced to retreat.

He had accomplished one purpose. He had convinced the Government that a new treaty was necessary to placate the hostile Sioux. In 1868 the Sioux tribes were summoned to Fort Laramie for negotiations. Representatives came from the Oglalas, Minneconjou, Yanktonnais, Arapahoes, Hunkpapa, Blackfeet, Cutheads, Two Kettles, Sans Arc, Santee, which included most of the Sioux nation. The treaty which they signed established the boundaries of the great Sioux reservation, encouraged the Indians to become farmers, promised agency buildings for each reservation, education, and agricultural needs for all those who would engage in farming, besides a sum of money and annuity goods to be paid each year to the Indians taking part in the treaty.

Red Cloud demurred. He refused to sign until the three forts on the Bozeman Trail were destroyed, Fort Phil Kearny, Fort C. F. Smith and Fort Reno. Red Cloud led a great force of warriors by that time. Government officials agreed. The three forts would be discontinued.

Red Cloud signed, but before the troopers rode from sight of Fort Phil Kearny, the Sioux warrior Little Wolf set fire to the buildings. The Bozeman Trail was abandoned.

American Horse, Oglala warrior, accompanied Red Cloud to Washington during several delegations, and appeared to be in attendance at most treaty councils. He was in Washington in 1874 to discuss Black Hills cession possibilities, in 1877, 1880, and again in 1891 after the Wounded Knee affair to plead for his people. (Photo by courtesy of Smithsonian Institution, National Anthropological Archives)

Red Dog, Oglala warrior, accompanied Red Cloud to Washington on some occasions, notably in 1875 when Red Dog was one of the speakers attempting to hold hostile tempers in line when discussing the Black Hills treaty. (Photo by courtesy of Smithsonian Institution National Anthropological Archives)

Believing that he had accomplished his purpose, Red Cloud agreed to live in peace. The treaty had given the Sioux

"all the lands in the Territory of Dakota south of the Cannon Ball River and west of the Missouri." [1]

It seemed enough at the time. The question remained of where Red Cloud would live. He suggested that he would be quite happy to continue trading at Fort Laramie, but that fort was not an Indian reservation. Red Cloud and his people left for the Powder River, but returned to Fort Laramie whenever they needed rations. They were fed, still waiting for a definite agency for the Red Cloud Oglalas.

In 1870 Red Cloud announced that he was going to Washington to meet the President. Spotted Tail was already in the city. The two men were not on friendly terms at the moment inasmuch as Spotted Tail had killed Big Mouth, an Oglala chief and personal friend of Red Cloud, in a hand to hand fight at Whetstone Agency only the year previously, 1869, but when they met in Washington they were polite to each other.

Red Cloud arrived June 3, and they were conducted to the Interior Department for an interview. Indian Commissioner Parker welcomed them with Secretary of the Interior Cox. Red Cloud was anxious to speak. He demanded a few "wagon loads of ammunition," [2] which were denied under the supposition that the Indians should be keeping peace with the whites, and such large amounts of ammunition were unnecessary. Red Cloud demanded that the government remove Fort Fetterman, and refused permission to build roads through the Black Hills and the Big Horns. He accused the President of failure in giving the Red Cloud lodges a reservation where he wanted it, failure to give him traders, failure to

General Crook's army in camp at Point of Rocks near Buffalo Gap, Black Hills, 1870's. General Crook kept a sharp eye on Red Cloud after the cession of the Black Hills, with numerous reports that Red Cloud was harassing the whites. (Photo from the Morrow Collection, by courtesy of the University of South Dakota Museum)

Issue day at Pine Ridge, winter. When Red Cloud decided to accept an agency of his own and for his Oglala followers, first near Camp Robinson and later at Pine Ridge, part of the terms were that the federal government would issue beef and supplies at certain periods of each year. (Photo by courtesy of Smithsonian Institution, National Anthropological Archives)

negotiate with him for railroads through his lands, and accused people sent to him at his camp as liars. Spotted Tail spoke with less animosity, supporting the half breed John Richard who had been accused of murder and asking for leniency.

On June 11 they held a final council. Secretary Cox suggested that Red Cloud did not fully understand the 1868 treaty. In the discussion which followed Red Cloud suddenly lifted his hands in a gesture toward the Great Spirit, and said:

"The Great Spirit is now looking at us and we offer our prayers . . .
You made a chief of Conquering Bear and then destroyed him, and since then we have had no more chiefs . . . You have the names to the treaty of persons professing to be chiefs, but I am chief of that nation . . . ." [3]

He had no further business with them, he said, and demanded to be put on the railroad to go back to his home.

The *New York Standard* and the *New York Times* reporters were impressed with the speeches made by Red Cloud, and said so. The *New York Tribune* spoke of

"the remarkable triumph of Red Cloud yesterday in the great speech he delivered before the assembled multitude at Cooper Institute. . . ." [4]

but the *New York Herald* saw the whole incident as a preliminary to another war by Red Cloud and his people.

In June of 1871 Red Cloud and his Oglalas conferred with the Board of Indian Commissioners at Fort Laramie on the subject of his permanent reservation site. After palavering around the subject, arguing for and against various sites, Red Cloud still refused to actually name a desired site. Nothing would persuade him to state a definite suggestion, but when the council was over Red Cloud said quietly to Commissioner Felix R. Brunot, "I am willing to go over the river but I want all the rest to agree to it . . . . I was afraid to say so but the rest will come to it." [5]

So the council was wasted time. Red Cloud continued to camp at Fort Laramie whenever they wanted food.

The Indian Commissioners were trying to persuade Red Cloud to accept an agency at Raw Hide Buttes, about 40 miles north of Fort Laramie, but Red Cloud refused to be interested. He kept his 1500 people near Fort Laramie. It

Dr. Valentine T. McGillycuddy, agent at Pine Ridge Indian Agency between 1879-1886. McGillycuddy and Red Cloud held a continuing feud until Red Cloud's protests finally were instrumental in McGillycuddy's transfer elsewhere. (Photo from South Dakota Historical Society)

Little Wound, Oglala warrior, attended some of the Washington delegations with Red Cloud (Photo by courtesy of Smithsonian Institution, National Anthropological Archives)

was 1872 before the problem was settled. When Red Cloud persisted in not naming a site, Agent J. W. Daniels notified him that the new Red Cloud Agency would be on the White River, and if they wanted goods delivered to them that would be where they would find them. The ultimatum was accepted, and Red Cloud moved his people to the upper White River, a spot near Fort Robinson which was built a little later.

Having moved, Red Cloud announced that he was going to Washington. He took twenty six warriors with him, but nothing of moment was accomplished by the delegation.

Red Cloud and his Oglalas were not the only unhappy Sioux on the western prairies. Generally speaking, the great Sioux nation resented a proposed expedition of 1872 from Sioux City to the Black Hills, they resented the telegraph line to Fort Sully because nobody had asked permission of the Indians to cross their lands, they resented the Northern Pacific Railroad building across Indian territory, and they spoke bitterly of high prices charged by traders in trading stores.

The entire Indian question on the prairies began to move toward a head in 1873 and 1874 when rumors of gold in the Black Hills began to circulate widely. The time was ripe for a new gold rush, and the fact that the Black Hills was in the center of the great Sioux reservation was small deterrent to the eager miners waiting to get into the hills with their prospectors' pans and shovels. General George A. Custer was sent from Fort Abraham Lincoln in the summer of 1874 with a magnificent entourage of a thousand men and provisions to match. He entered the Black Hills from the west, moved soutwest toward his so-called Permanent Camp near the present town of Custer where his men found gold colors on French Creek, took several days to explore the surrounding mountains and climb to the top of the towering Harney Peak, then moved northeast to the edge of the Black Hills and back to Fort Lincoln in present North Dakota. He reported the truth as he found it—there was indeed gold in the Black Hills.

But the Black Hills was Indian land! The Sioux were not eager to lose their hills, and they said so in no uncertain terms.

The Government asked the Agents at Red Cloud Agency, Spotted Tail's Agency, and Cheyenne Agency to bring a delegation of the strongest Indian chiefs to Washington for an interview in 1874 to discuss the matter. Sixteen Oglalas headed by Red Cloud and Man Afraid of His Horses were in the group. Four Brules were led by Spotted Tail. Seven Minneconjous and nine Cheyennes including the man Charger who was later to become famous for his own leadership were in the band. They arrived in Washington May 18, and met President Grant the next day.

The purpose of the interview was to make a treaty for the transfer of the Black Hills from the Indian reservation to the public domain, and for the granting of right of way for wagon roads from the Missouri River across the Sioux Reservation to the Black Hills. Spotted Tail was recognized as speaker for the Sioux, and he urged that white miners be kept out of the Black Hills until an honorable settlement could be made.

"It will take a heap of money," [6] he said, to buy the Black Hills, knowing that the land was valuable for its mineral content to the whites, far more valuable than its intrinsic value to the red men.

The conference settled nothing.

In the Black Hills, government geologist Walter P. Jenney and his party went into the Black Hills in the spring of 1875 to certify the fact of gold in the streams. It was there. Something had to be done. The Sioux were invited back to Washington for further discussion.

According to historian George W. Kingsbury:

"The visit of the Sioux to Washington in 1875 had apprised them that the Government contemplated their removal to the Indian Territory, and they were advised to consider it; it also revealed a willingness on the part of the Indians to treat for a cession of the Black Hills country. Their general conduct, however, was unlike that habitually displayed by the Indians when visiting Washington; they were disposed to be arrogant, and paid little attention to proprieties in their behavior. They appeared to feel that they were masters of an important situation in which they held the whites and the Government at their command." [7]

A report was circulated that the Indians intended to kill a commissioner while in Washington. Red Cloud, Spotted Tail, Young Man Afraid of His Horses and other friendly chiefs managed to keep their men in line. Red Dog spoke for the Oglalas, and Spotted Tail spoke for the Brules during the first day, outlining

Pine Ridge Agency in the 1880's. (Photo from South Dakota Historical Society)

Young Man Afraid of His Horses, son of Man Afraid of His Horses, chief of the Oglalas. Young Man Afraid and Red Cloud were on opposite sides of the progressive movement led by Agent V. T. McGillycuddy 1879-1886. (Photo by courtesy of Smithsonian Institute, National Anthropological Archives)

their demands for Black Hills cession. Red Cloud spoke the next day, wasting no words.

"I consider the hills more valuable in precious metals than the entire wealth of the United States, and I propose to ask a large sum for them, the principal to be put to interest, and get enough interest to keep the whole Sioux nation." [8]

He outlined the Sioux demands, including materials, money, removal of troops, the right to appoint their own Indian agents, employees and traders, and no more roads into the Black Hills territory, with the land being considered in treaty only

"such portions of the Black Hills country as contains gold." [9]

In this, Red Cloud was supported by almost the entire Sioux delegation.

The commisssioners presented their treaty, and though there was a polite discussion of its contents, the Sioux would have none of it. Treaty making for the Black Hills was terminated for the moment, and the Sioux returned to the western prairies.

Only Spotted Tail made any pretense of considering the idea thoughtfully. With Red Cloud so obdurantly against cession, General Crook announced that Red Cloud would no longer be considered head chief of all Sioux tribes. Spotted Tail was given the honor, if honor it was by that time.

Miners slipped into the Black Hills without permission immediately after Custer's return, and by 1875 they were entrenched on the streams of the hills in spite of the fact that military men were ordering them out of Indian territory as fast as they could catch them. President Grant had issued a proclamation early in the year, January 11, 1875, withdrawing a large area of lands in Dakota from market and specifying such lands for the use of the Indians only. The Sioux reservation already covered a huge territory west of the Missouri River. The lands in the new proclamation were east of the Missouri River, which gave the Sioux nearly one half of the Territory of Dakota. The purpose of such a reservation, it was stated, was to place the country under control of the Department of the Interior, thus making it easier to control liquor in Indian country. That the purpose was not accomplished was evident in the restoration of all such withdrawn lands to public domain by President Hayes, August 9, 1879, four years later.

Secretary Chandler of the Interior Department recommended the removal of the Red Cloud and Spotted Tail bands to the Missouri River in that troubled year of 1875. It would be easier to supply their annuity goods on the banks of the Missouri river rather than transport them inland. Neither Red Cloud nor Spotted Tail liked the idea, not one whit.

White leaders and Indians on the Pine Ridge Agency during the leadership of Agent V. T. McGilly-cuddy, 1880's. (Photo from South Dakota Historical Society)

The year 1876 started with the proclamation of the president that all Indians in the Sioux Reservation should take residence on the agencies by January 31, 1876, or be considered hostiles. No sensible Indian traveled in the wintertime, and that winter was a cold one. The Sioux paid no attention to the order. Lt. General Philip H. Sheridan was given the job of bringing the Sioux to the Agencies, and with the aid of Brig. General Alfred H. Terry, Col. John Gibbon, and Brig. General George Crook he made plans.

In Powder River country the Sioux tribes were gathering from all directions, though Sitting Bull, Hunkpapa medicine man, insisted later that the great gathering of Sioux had nothing to do with the presidential order or war parties. It was, he said, an annual gathering of Sioux for a social meeting that the young men of the tribes could find wives in other Sioux tribes—a traditional spring festival of sorts. Whatever it was, General Terry found the wide Indian trail and followed it.

Whether the Battle of the Little Big Horn on June 16, 1876 which resulted from the meeting of the military and the Sioux could have been avoided or not has been argued by western historians since that day, but the end result was the death of General George Armstrong Custer and his entire Seventh Cavalry on a desolate hillside in the Big Horn Mountains.

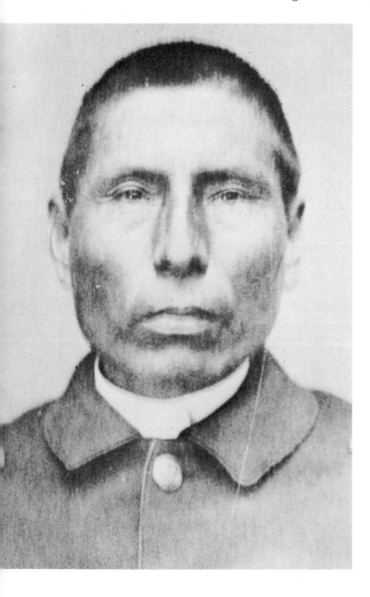

Captain Sword, chief of the Indian police on Pine Ridge Agency during McGillycuddy's agency, 1879-1886. (Photo by courtesy of the Smithsonian Institution, National Anthropological Archives)

Oglala delegation to Washington, 1880. Seated, left to right, Red Dog, Little Wound, Red Cloud, American Horse, Red Shirt; standing, John Bridgeman. The 1880 delegation was there for another of Red Cloud's complaints against Agent V. T. McGillycuddy, but the delegation accomplished nothing of great moment, and they returned to Pine Ridge. (Photo by courtesy of Smithsonian Institution, National Anthropological Archives)

Sitting Bull was there. Crazy Horse, the young warrior, was very much part of the action. Gall, the fighting cock of the Hunkpapas, was in the thick of the battle. Some three thousand Indians, more or less, were in that bloody battlefield, but Red Cloud was not. He was safely entrenched in his Agency near Fort Robinson. Though he had been encouraging his men to fight the whites, he himself had no part in General Custer's famous demise.

When the dead were counted and the wounded carried back to civilization on the steamer *Far West,* the United States Government moved with no further delay. President Grant appointed a commission to draw a new treaty, and they intended this to be signed by the Sioux with no more quibbling.

The commission met at Omaha, Nebraska August 28, 1876, then proceeded to Red Cloud Agency September 7 to meet the Sioux. Red Cloud's name was first on the list of signers, and his name was followed by Man Afraid of His Horses and many others. Spotted Tail's name led the Brules. The Lower and Upper Yanctonnais signed, the Hunkpapas, Blackfeet, Sans Arc, Two Kettles, Minneconjou, Brules and Santee all signed. The Black Hills was opened for settlement.

September 9, two days later, the battle of Slim Buttes occurred north of the Black Hills. Some said Crazy Horse led that battle, others said Crazy Horse was miles distant and the battle was encouraged by Red Cloud and his "refractory people." [10]

Sioux began harassing and killing people going into the Black Hills, and again Red Cloud was blamed. Newspaper accounts stated baldly that Indian raiders belonged to Red Cloud's band. White men were killed. Covered wagons were ambushed and burned. The Sioux considered that they had been forced to deed the Black Hills to the whites, and they did not like it.

Crazy Horse and Sitting Bull were openly termed hostiles after the Battle of the Little Big Horn. Sitting Bull fled to Canada with his people, safe from the military as long as he stayed there. Crazy Horse and his Oglalas were hiding in Powder River country, but Red Cloud and his Oglalas remained on the Agency. General Crook had no trust for Red Cloud in spite of appearances. He announced peremptorily that Spotted Tail would forthwith be the new chief of all Indians, leader of the Red Cloud Agency as well as the Spotted Tail Agency. Red Cloud was furious.

It was necessary to bring the hostiles to terms. Crook asked Spotted Tail to go to Crazy Horse with an offer of welcome from the government officers at Red Cloud Agency. Lt. W. P. Clark sent Red Cloud on the same mission and Red Cloud was pleased to go, but it was Spotted Tail, Crazy Horse's uncle, who persuaded the young warrior to lead his people to the Red Cloud Agency in the spring of 1877. The cold winter had been a factor. The hunger of the hostile Oglalas was another reason. Red Cloud met him, and Crazy Horse came in, leading his people one thousand strong, singing as they came to the Agency.

Peace might have come then, but mistrust was everywhere on the Agency grounds. When the Sioux themselves began to whisper dangerous things about Crazy Horse, the warrior was arrested and brought to the Fort Robinson jail. In his effort to escape, Crazy Horse was killed by his own Sioux friends, or enemies whichever they might be called.

Removal of the Red Cloud and Spotted Tail Sioux to the Missouri River had been considered since 1875. After the murder of Crazy Horse the Indian Commissioners decided that they had waited too long. Both chiefs were ordered to move their people to the Missouri River, though they protested mightily.

In September 1877 Red Cloud and Spotted Tail headed delegations of the Sioux and Arapahoe Indians in a visit to Washington to protest. Red Cloud asked for a site at the foot of the Black Hills for his agency. Spotted Tail stated that he would not allow his people to live on the Missouri River, regardless of orders. They managed one concession. They must stay on the Missouri River through the winter of 1877, they were told, but when spring came their requests for an inland reservation would be given consideration

In the spring Red Cloud led his people west. His site was at Pine Ridge, well to his liking. Spotted Tail's Brules settled on the Rosebud.

Dr. Valentine T. McGillycuddy was appointed Agent at the Pine Ridge Agency in 1879, and with his coming Red Cloud began a new war. McGillycuddy was a young man. Red Cloud was 57 and becoming more bitter as he grew older. McGillycuddy wanted to introduce new ways to Pine Ridge Agency, and did so though Red Cloud fought him every step of the way.

McGillycuddy caught the situation immediately. He learned that Red Cloud had been a warrior chief only, that Red Cloud was not a hereditary chief such as Young Man Afraid of His Horses. Somehow he learned that Young Man Afraid, American Horse, and Sword, young men all, had been the Shirt Wearers of that Oglala ceremony a few years previously and that Red Cloud had been only a warrior stand-in while Young Man Afraid was growing to maturity. McGillycuddy called Red Cloud "the usurper" [11] and recognized Young Man Afraid as the "rightful chieftain" [12] whose support he could trust in his efforts to improve the status of the Sioux at Pine Ridge. The line between the two Sioux was sharply drawn, Red Cloud stubborn in his refusal to cooperate, Young Man

Red Cloud, chief of the Oglala Sioux, under arrest at Fort Robinson in 1882. (Photo from the Morrow Collection, by courtesy of the University of South Dakota Museum)

Afraid working toward progressive civilization even as McGillycuddy was getting acquainted with his new job. The *Black Hills Journal,* published in Deadwood August 23, 1879, presented the full speech of Young Man Afraid while the young Oglala was in the little frontier town of Rapid City, Dakota Territory on the edge of the Black Hills.

Young Man Afraid was a powerful speaker. He stated flatly that he was a friend of the whites and wanted to do what he could to help the Sioux find peace with the white men.

"I know many good white people work with me, and try to help me," he said. "We want to be peaceable forever—as long as the grass grow and the winds blow." [13]

McGillycuddy learned of that speach, and appreciated it.

He also recognized George Sword as a man on whom he could lean. When he suggested Indian police on the reservation rather than military white men, he appointed Sword their Captain. Red Cloud objected, saying they needed no Indian police. Sword, with McGillycuddy's permission, arranged a beef barbecue for the police, and Red Cloud led a marauding party and stole the beef.

When Secretary of the Interior Schurz visited Pine Ridge, McGillycuddy called a grand council of the principal men at the Agency. Red Cloud wore his black broadcloth suit as evidence of his status, while Young Man Afraid was content with a blue blanket and a single eagle's feather. Red Cloud held the peace pipe at arm's length and called for the guidance of the Great Spirit with his arms upraised. When the pipe had made the rounds, Red Cloud made his speech. He wanted payment for land, more annuities and rations, wagons, cows, other animals, and many other articles. That done, he listed the things that he did not want. He did not want McGillycuddy. He did not want the Indian police.

Young Man Afraid spoke with praise of the work being done by McGillycuddy. The Secretary rebuked Red Cloud mildly, and after examination of the Pine Ridge affairs reported that McGillycuddy was doing a good job.

Red Cloud's animosity toward McGillycuddy remained. Continually he petitioned for a new agent, and always McGillycuddy was exonerated of Red Cloud's accusations. The Indian police force thrived under Captain Sword. Gradually the progressive policies of Young Man Afraid augmented McGillycuddy's advice in every way, while Red Cloud grumbled. McGillycuddy seemed to be winning, yet at any moment he knew that Red Cloud was hatching some new deviltry to harass him.

Spotted Tail could see what was happening at Pine Ridge and attempted to advise Red Cloud:

> "Take my advice, Brother Red Cloud, and don't fight against this boy the Great Father has sent to be your agent. He knows what is best for the Indian. If you don't do as he says, he'll break you up, Brother Red Cloud." [14]

Red Cloud laughed in disgust. He began going to Washington with his querulous accusations, back to Pine Ridge, to Washington again. McGillycuddy did not try to stop him. When the Commission of Indian Affairs summoned him to answer Red Cloud's denunciations, McGillycuddy cleared himself of every question. Still Red Cloud snarled in his home, watching for some way to discredit McGillycuddy.

Spotted Tail was killed by Crow Dog, a member of his own band, in 1881. It was a great loss to the neighboring Brules, and a loss of friendship to Red Cloud in spite of the differences between the two leaders. Spotted Tail and Red Cloud had been contemporaries, and Red Cloud could see younger men taking the leadership that he felt belonged to him.

Sitting Bull surrendered from his self imposed exile in 1881 and became a prisoner at Fort Yates. Red Cloud knew the old ways of the nomadic Sioux had changed, but he would not yield. Some way, he told himself, he would yet win.

In 1882 Red Cloud determined to make a last stand against his enemy, McGillycuddy. For three years he had fought him. He threatened to kill McGillycuddy and Mrs. McGillycuddy.

McGillycuddy called a council of his supporters at Pine Ridge. News of the trouble reached Washington, and offers of help came to McGillycuddy over telegraph lines, but McGillycudddy was sure he could handle the situation by himself.

Red Cloud was summoned. With several hundred blanketed Indians, Red Cloud filled the council room. Sword and his Indian police kept an anxious eye on them. The situation was tense when one of Red Cloud's men bellowed, "There sits your chief. Stand by him."[15]

McGillycuddy began talking, speaking of the many times he had tried to tell Red Cloud of the ways in which he wanted to help the Oglalas, and the many times that Red Cloud would not listen. Red Cloud would no longer be considered any more than a subchief, McGillycuddy said, and would be further demoted if he persisted in trouble.

"Never again shall I recognize you as head chief," he said. "I depose you!" [16]

He showed the telegram which he had just received from the Commissioner, which stated:

> "You may arrest Red Cloud and hold him prisoner if necessary to preserve the peace." [17]

Spotted Tail, Brule chief, cautioned Red Cloud that he should try to cooperate with Agent McGillycuddy when the feud was at its hottest, but Red Cloud would not listen to Spotted Tail. (Photo by courtesy of Nebraska State Historical Society)

Jack Red Cloud, son of Red Cloud, did not attain the prominence that his father had held. (Photo by courtesy of Smithsonian Institution, National Anthropological Archives)

Before Red Cloud's followers could take any organized action, McGillycuddy ordered that the council be cleared. He had won for the day.

Red Cloud asked permission to visit Washington again and McGillycuddy allowed him to do so. He returned with no results. Nevertheless he had not given up his plan to get rid of McGillycuddy. He concocted tricks with younger malcontents, hoping to trap McGillycuddy some way. His tricks did not work. He turned his influence to white men's newspapers of the east, and as reports from Red Cloud continued to lambast McGillycuddy, the Indian Ring in the east began to believe the old Sioux.

The breach between the two men was permanent. McGillycuddy was called to Washington to answer Red Cloud's charges. Red Cloud was there, wearing his black broadcloth suit. Young Man Afraid accompanied McGillycuddy, and Captain Sword watched with both of them. The trial was extensive, but it came to nothing as usual.

Again McGillycuddy was investigated at Red Cloud's demands. He became known as the most investigated agent in Indian territory, and finally in May 1886 he was relieved of his duties in the interest of peace. He was given the position of Assistant Adjutant General for the United States Army, and Red Cloud had his way. He had a new agent on Pine Ridge, Captain James M. Bell, who was succeeded October 1 by H. D. Gallagher. The quarreling on Pine Ridge Reservation became quiet, and by the middle of the next year Red Cloud and Young Man Afraid had agreed to cooperate with each other.

Pine Ridge Agency was officially declared an Indian Reservation in 1889, the year before the great Messiah Craze swept the Indian nation in western lands. From the Mississippi River to the western seacoast the Indians were in a mood for a religious revival. When Wavoka, a young Ute Indian, declared himself the Messiah come to bring back the old ways of Indians, the buffalo to return and the white men to vanish, it seemed like the words of the Great Spirit himself. Part of the Messiah Craze was the wearing of ghost shirts which were said to be impervious to the bullets of the white soldiers, and a ghost dance which spread like wildfire.

Sitting Bull on his Standing Rock Reservation on the borderline between present day South and North Dakota sponsored the Messiah dancing with all the strength he had. The military men mistrusted the new craze. It was too soon to forget the frenzy of the killing in the Battle of the Little Big Horn. They ordered Sitting Bull to report to military authorities in 1890, but Sitting Bull was killed by the Indian police who went to get him.

Red Cloud, Oglala war chief.
(Photo from South Dakota
Historical Society)

Sitting Bull's people fled to join Big Foot's band as they moved through the Bad Lands of South Dakota, seeking Red Cloud. Big Foot said that Red Cloud had invited him to come for a council, that only with Red Cloud would he be safe. Big Foot was met and escorted by the military men to Wounded Knee. In a misunderstanding and panic, the white soldiers began firing into the Indian camp. The Wounded Knee massacre was unnecessary, unplanned, and bloody, the last big encounter between red men and white. The Messiah Craze stopped as suddenly as it began, and on the reservations the Sioux people moaned quietly among themselves.

In 1891 when the shock of Wounded Knee had somewhat quietened, Young Man Afraid, American Horse, Little Wound, Two Strike, Hump and other chiefs went to Washington again, this time to plead for their people and the suffering of the Indians. Red Cloud did not go. They had no need to plead. Wounded Knee was the last battle between the two races.

Red Cloud lived to be 87 years old. He died at Pine Ridge Indian Reservation December 10, 1909, an aged man resentful toward the whites until his death. His eyesight failed him in his later years, and his influence faded. He had been to Washington fifteen times, by his own count, and had done what he could for his Oglala people.

He was the last of the famous Sioux leaders who lived during the rebellion years of the prairie Indians. Crazy Horse had been murdered by his own people. Spotted Tail had taken the bullet of an assassin, a man who worked by his side. Sitting Bull had been killed by the Indian police when he resisted arrest. Gall had turned to the ways of the white men. Only Red Cloud had died an old man, old in years, old in ideas, a remnant of a civilization that was no more.

He had tried to cling to a pattern of life that had to change. He could not change with it, but his anger colored his life as long as he lived.

Who is to say whether he was right or wrong?

Quoted References: Red Cloud, the Schemer.

[1] Kingsbury, George W., *History of Dakota Territory,* Volume I. The S. J. Clarke Publishing Company, Chicago, Illinois, 1915. p. 767.

[2] "Digest of Indian Commissioner Reports," *South Dakota Historical Collections,* Volume XXVIII, 1956. South Dakota Historical Society, Pierre, South Dakota. p. 234.

[3] "Digest of Indian Commissioner Reports," Volume XXVIII, pp. 237-238.

[4] "Digest of Indian Commissioner Reports," Volume XXVIII, p. 241.

[5] "Digest of Indian Commissioner Reports," Volume XXVIII, p. 290.

[6] Kingsbury, opus cited, p. 900.

[7] Kingsbury, opus cited, p. 912.

[8] Kingsbury, opus cited, p. 914.

[9] Kingsbury, opus cited, p. 915.

[10] Kingsbury, opus cited, p. 958.

[11] McGillycuddy, Julia B., *McGillycuddy: Agent.* Stanford University Press, Stanford, California 1941. p. 6.

[12] McGillycuddy, opus cited, p.6.

[13] "Let the Young Men Rule Was Plea of Sioux Chief," *Rapid City Journal,* September 28, 1969. Rapid City, South Dakota.

[14] McGillycuddy, opus cited, p. 182.

[15] McGillycuddy, opus cited, p. 195.

[16] McGillycuddy, opus cited, p. 196.

[17] McGillycuddy, opus cited, p. 195.

7

CHAUNCEY YELLOW ROBE, BRIDGE BETWEEN TWO CULTURES.

The Indian warriors came into camp tired. They had ridden for days, and they had just come from the Battle of the Little Big Horn. The details of that fierce fight were still in their minds as they rode into their home camp, and it lifted them with a profound pride that at last they had struck a decisive blow for their homeland, their families, and their way of living.

Chauncey Yellow Robe was a small boy only six years old, but he was old enough to remember them. He saw the Indian men pull their ponies to a stop, slide off in the easy grace of the plains horseman, and stand erect and tall as they told of the battle. Custer had been killed, the famed Yellow Hair who led his soldiers against them from one end of the plains to another. Every one of Custer's men had died with him, the warriors said. Some of them showed scalps which they had taken from the dead. Others had rifles, bayonets, pistols which they had brought as spoils of war.

Nearly fifty years later, Chauncey remembered that day and he told the story over a newfangled contraption called radio which was being developed in the Black Hills and the United States. Fifty years were a long time when he considered all that had happened between that day in 1876 and the afternoon in the 1920's when he talked on the radio.

It is easy to remember the names of Sitting Bull, Crazy Horse, Spotted Tail, Red Cloud and some of the other Sioux chiefs who made history during the days when the Sioux were fighting the gradual encroachment of whites in the land of the Dakotas. The word Dakotah meant the largest division of the Sioux Indians in the nineteenth century, and the Sioux roamed over the western and northern prairies in a wild free state.

Eventually the west was conquered. The proud Sioux found themselves on reservations—the Pine Ridge, Rosebud, Sisseton, Crow Creek and others—and the problem then was to learn how to live with the white men. In the years that followed, one of the greatest Indian leaders was Chauncey Yellow Robe, Disciplinarian at the United States Indian School at Rapid City, South Dakota for 25 years, and speaker for his people, representing them at ceremonies of dignity, leader of the Sioux and a link with the white ways of living needed when the Dakotahs were trying to understand civilization.

Chauncey Yellow Robe bridged a generation. He knew what it was to shoot buffalo from an Indian pony with only a bow and arrow. He was one of the first Sioux Indians to attend Carlisle University, Pennsylvania, and to be graduated with honors from that government school for Indians, and he tried to educate the young men and women who followed him.

Is he worth knowing? He is, indeed.

They called him the "Sioux spokesman."[1] He was the Sioux champion no matter where he worked, where he spoke, where he lived.

Sixty years ago he wrote a review of his boyhood. He was born on the prairies (he thinks in southern Montana) and with his people, the *Lacota oyate* or Sioux nation, he roamed the plains of South and North Dakota, Nebraska, Wyoming and Montana. Son of a hereditary chief *Tasinagi*, or Yellow Robe, and his mother *Tahcawin* (Female Deer) who was the niece of Sitting Bull, Chauncey began with the name *Conowicakte* (Kill in Woods). He killed his first buffalo while still a boy:

"I picked up my arrow quiver and a piece of buffalo raw hide rope and running to the ponies on the field caught my fleet footed pony and

Chauncey Yellow Robe in the costume he wore for the filming of the movie *The Silent Enemy*, produced in New York 1929. (Photo by Della B. Vik)

joined the hunting party. When we were out five or six miles from the camp we saw the buffalo herd, something like two or three thousand, calves and all, grazing on a broad stretch of low land. We made an advance towards the buffaloes behind the hills and then we made charge upon them, shouting war whoops as we went. The great buffalo herd stampeded towards the west, a thick cloud of dust rising behind them. My pony was so excited that I could not control him. Reaching the buffaloes through the smoke of dust, I was right among them. They rubbed against my side as they ran.

"My pony turned his ears down and raced with the herd. I was afraid at first, thinking if I fell off my pony I would be tramped to death by the buffaloes. Finally I gained confidence in myself and drew my bow and arrows out from the quiver at my belt and sent the first arrow into a yearling buffalo on my right. She staggered and dropped out of the stampede, and so I shot another arrow into her. My last

Indian killing buffalo. (Painting by Karl Bodmer, 1834, courtesy of American Museum, New York)

arrow was effective. She finally lay down and died, killed with the bow and arrows I myself had made. With much pleasurable emotions within my heart to see the dead buffalo before me, I dismounted and tied my pony to a sagebrush and skinned the buffalo the way my father and uncle had taught me to do." [2]

When Chauncey was fifteen General R. H. Pratt, the founder of Carlisle University, took him to Carlisle. The young Indian boy was terribly homesick at first, but in the next ten years of schooling he not only learned to enjoy the school but he graduated with honors in the class of 1895. He entered the school service under the government.

Whether he returned to South Dakota immediately is not certain, but he was appointed Disciplinarian for the United States Indian School at Rapid City around 1903, only eight years after his graduation from Carlisle. He held that position (actually boys' advisor) for the next 25 years, and with it he became one of the most respected and well known Indian leaders in South Dakota.

A photograph of Chauncey and his family was published in that 1915 brochure showing his wife and two small daughters, Rosebud aged about eight in the picture and Chauncina perhaps five years old. This would suggest that he married around 1905. His wife was a delicate and refined French Canadian nurse. Rosebud was a pretty child, and as she grew older she became more graceful and beautiful.

By 1913 Chauncey was already a spokesman for his Sioux people. While visiting in the eastern states on a mission, he heard that the famous western scout, Buffalo Bill Cody, was backing a motion picture showing the Wounded Knee massacre of 1890. The movie was being shot at the Pine Ridge Agency, South Dakota, beginning October 11, 1913. Buffalo Bill was himself acting in the movie, and various Indians and military men who had been at Wounded Knee on

114

Buffalo Bill (William F. Cody). Buffalo Bill took part in a movie on the battle of Wounded Knee, photographed in the Pine Ridge Agency during 1913, which Chauncey resented because of its exploitation. (Photo from the collection of S. Goodale Price)

Chauncey Yellow Robe as a young man. (Photo from *Rapid City Holiday Greetings*, 1915)

the fateful day had been invited to participate in the movie version. It was planned that the movie be authentic, so authentic that it was to be filed among the historical archives of the War Department when finished.

The story of Wounded Knee has been told and retold. It began with the dream of a Messiah who would drive the whites from Indian territory, bring back the buffalo and remake the country into the happy hunting ground of former days. Dancing being the natural religious expression for the Indians, a dance characterized by a ghost shirt said to protect the wearer from bullets was part of the ceremony. As the Messianic ghost shirt dancing spread over the west, white men began to panic.

The first big mistake was the killing of Sitting Bull. His followers ran, joining the Minneconjous under Big Foot who were moving through the South Dakota Bad Lands. Big Foot and his group were apprehended by the Seventh Cavalry and conducted to a spot called Wounded Knee, heavily guarded by military men. Big Foot did not fight, he was sick with pneumonia and had hoisted the white flag of truce.

Though many errors were compounded in the ghost dance craze, the big mistake was the firing of a single shot by somebody at Wounded Knee. Pandemonium broke loose. Soldiers fired into the helpless Indian camp. When the firing stopped, nearly 300 men, women and children of Chief Big Foot's band lay dead in the snow of that December 1890 morning, including Big Foot himself, and between thirty and forty troopers were killed.

115

Rapid City, South Dakota, 1902. (Photo by E. D. McNamara)

A South Dakota blizzard struck that night. When they could get back to the frozen bodies the military men buried 120 Indians in a mass grave at Wounded Knee.

The memory remains, a mockery of judgement on the part of the whites, the Indians, the agents, the chiefs, the soldiers, the generals, anybody and everybody involved. It was the last great clash between the red and white man.

Regardless of how the whites felt about that battle, the Indians were understandably bitter. They had been in camp with a white flag raised for truce. They were not attacking the soldiers, but were dancing only in a religious ceremony.

When Chauncey Yellow Robe heard about the movie he was in Albany, New York, attending a meeting of the Society of American Indians. He began with a few

"terse and cutting phrases . . ." [3]

which flayed Colonel William F. Cody and General Nelson A. Miles for the part they played in the recent reenactment of the Battle of Wounded Knee for the benefit of a moving picture concern. He reminded his Indian companions that Buffalo Bill and General Miles had not even been at Wounded Knee at the time. He accused them of exploiting the event for their own glory. In a report from the Albany newspaper, Chauncey's words became bitter as he continued:

"You ask how to settle the Indian troubles . . . . I have a suggestion. Let Buffalo Bill and General Miles take some soldiers and go around the reservations and shoot them down. That will settle his troubles. Let them do in earnest what they have been doing at the battlefield at Wounded Knee. These two, who were not even there when it happen-

116

Chauncey Yellow Robe,
Mrs. Yellow Robe, and
daughters Rosebud and
Chauncina at the time when
he was Disciplinarian at
the United States Indian
School, Rapid City, South
Dakota, 1915. (From *Rapid
City Holiday Greetings*,
1915)

117

Main school building at the United States Indian School, Rapid City, South Dakota, 1915. (Photo from *Rapid City Holiday Greetings*, 1915)

ed, went back and became heroes for a moving picture machine. You laugh, but my heart does not laugh. Women and children and old men of my people, my relatives, were massacred with machine guns by soldiers of this Christian nation while the fighting men were away. That was bad—bad for the Sioux and bad for the white man. It was not a glorious battle, and I should think these two men would be glad they were not there; but no, they want to be heroes for moving pictures. You will be able to see their bravery and their hair-breadth escapes soon in your theaters."[4]

Chauncey had been twenty years old at the time of the Wounded Knee battle, in school at Carlisle University. Though details of the battle were carefully followed, the picture was not a great success.

Mrs. Yellow Robe died in 1922, and with her death Chauncey suffered a great loss. A quiet white woman who had been devoted to her family, she had bridged the gap between her white culture and the Indian traditions to the benefit of her husband Chauncey, and their children. Four children had been born to them, Rosebud, Chauncina (1914), Chauncey, Jr. and Evelyn (1922). Rosebud would have been around eleven at the time of her death, the other children progressively younger. With the help of Chauncey's friends and relatives the children were loved, protected, and raised to maturity, but they must have missed their gentle mother through the years.

Indeed, Chauncey Yellow Robe had the respect of the town of Rapid City and of all who knew him in the state of South Dakota and over the United States where he was called to give speeches for the Sioux nation at various times. He was a member of the Masonic Lodge in Rapid City, accepted by the city's business men as one of them. It was because of that respect that he was asked to talk on an experimental radio station being operated by the South Dakota School of Mines in Rapid City. What happened is remembered with affection by the people in the surrounding Black Hills to this day.

Radio in the 1920's was still in its experimental stages, with programs often originating live in front of the microphones. This gave a certain unexpectedness to what came out of the few receiver sets in the area, but also served to make rabid fans of radio listeners. In following its policy of interviewing occasional well known people, station WCAT persuaded Chauncey to talk. Chauncey was somewhat wary of the idea at first, but as the boys from WCAT described the honor of talking to people not only in Rapid City but also the nearby towns in the Black Hills, Chauncey agreed to try. He arrived with some trepidation, but as the interview proceeded Chauncey warmed to the conversation with enthusiasm.

He told his radio audience of his early experiences as an Indian boy shortly after the Custer battle at the Little Big Horn.

He was too young to fight in those days, but he remembered the warriors when they returned from battle, and he told of the way the Indians lived when the whites were trying to persuade them to live only on the reservations. As he remembered the old ways of life on the prairie, his nostalgia for boyhood days overpowered his emotions. Without warning, he suddenly lifted his voice in an Indian war whoop that split the ears of the technicians.

Boys' Dormitory, United States Indian School, Rapid City, South Dakota, 1915. (Photo from *Rapid City Holiday Greetings*, 1915)

Chauncey Yellow Robe, 1927, at the time of the Calvin Coolidge ceremony. (Photo by Della B. Vik, in *The Black Hills Engineer*, November 1927)

Whammy! The transmitter tube of the radio exploded under the strain. The station was off the air without benefit of explanation or goodbyes.

That was it.

The Indian war whoop was the last the eager listeners heard that day.[5]

In 1927 President Calvin A. Coolidge came to the Black Hills for a three months' stay, ostensibly a vacation, but he brought his staff with him, newspaper correspondents, secret service men, and naturally his wife. His son John joined them before they left for the east coast again. Actually the seat of government was moved to the Black Hills for the summer. They arrived June 15 and remained until September 9.

One of President Coolidge's great interests was the Sioux Indian, whose reservations were so close to the Black Hills and whose schools were in the Black Hills. On July 7 President and Mrs. Coolidge visited the United States Indian School in Rapid City. They met the students, investigated the school facilities, and were presented with gifts of Indian workmanship.

A month later President and Mrs. Coolidge were special guests at the Days of '76 celebration in Deadwood, and there the President was made an honorary member of the Sioux tribe. It was in connection with that ceremony that Chauncey Yellow Robe was again called into the spotlight.

On August 4, several hundred Indians dressed in ceremonial costumes for the occasion were present with thousands of other spectators. Henry Standing Bear, a full blooded Brule farmer and Carlisle graduate from Wamblee, South Dakota, addressed the President in the Sioux language, which was then translated to English:

"Mr. President, it is a great honor to us that you have come among us and into our camp. We have nothing to give but our national

120

Henry Standing Bear beginning the ceremony making President Coolidge High Chieftain of all the Sioux, in the Black Hills, South Dakota, 1927. Mrs. Coolidge wearing big hat, President Coolidge standing beside her, Chauncey Yellow Robe by the president. Henry Standing Bear stands next to the Army officer. (Photo by Rise, from *The Black Hills Engineer*, November 1927)

respect, receive you into our people as one of us, and confer upon you the honor place in our tribe left vacant by Sitting Bull, Spotted Tail and Red Cloud.

"It is fitting that we are here standing side by side as brothers on this historical ground which was the very part of these Black Hills for which our people have long struggled against the whites and made our people and your people enemies.

"We are here today as your people. In our relationship with your people our forefathers handed down to us the tale of certain lamented events like the Custer battle, but marked as memorials to high and worthy examples for a future relationship more enlightened.

"Today we are here together again, in an event which shall mark in our history and in which one of the greatest of American peoples shall pay their highest national respect to you, by adopting you into the tribe, making you their High Chief, giving you a name to uphold.

"Our fathers and chiefs, Sitting Bull, Spotted Tail and Red Cloud, may have made mistakes; but their hearts were brave and strong, their purposes honest and noble. They have long gone to their Happy Hunting Ground, and we call upon you, as our new High Chief, to take up their leadership and fulfill the same duty call from which they never did shrink, a duty to protect and help the weak."[6]

As Standing Bear closed his address, Rosebud Yellow Robe, Chauncey's daughter, a "beautiful Indian maiden of rare talent,"[7] placed the Sioux Indian warbonnet on Coolidge's head. The warbonnet had been made with great care to

121

Blue Feather, noted Sioux woman, presented Mrs. Coolidge with a pair of beaded moccasins. In front, left to right: Blue Feather, Mrs. Coolidge, President Coolidge, Rosebud Robe, Standing Bear, and Chauncey Yellow Robe. (Photo by Rise Studio, from *The Black Hills Engineer*, November 1927)

be worthy of the event, its eagle feathered double streamer circling his brow and falling down his back. President Coolidge accepted the warbonnet gravely, then shook the hand of Standing Bear in appreciation.

A wild yell of approval rose from the Indian spectators, and some of them began singing. When the demonstration had quieted, Yellow Robe stood. His background was perfect as a representative member of the Sioux. His great uncle was Sitting Bull. His father was a Brule of Spotted Tail's band. His mother was a Hunkpapa of Sitting Bull's band. He himself had proved to be a leader among the Sioux. In the quiet, he spoke:

> "It is the greatest honor to the Sioux Tribe of South Dakota to bestow upon you the emblem of the Sioux Nation in a war bonnet, and to welcome you to our tribe. We name you Leading Eagle, *Wamblee-Tokaha*. By this name you are to be known—King and the greatest Chief, which is signified by the bonnet and the name you bear.
>
> "I congratulate you in the name of the Sioux Nation, and express the hope that you will continue to guide the will of this Nation to its great destiny."[8]

A Sioux woman, Blue Feather, then presented Mrs. Coolidge with beaded moccasins which she accepted graciously. Yellow Robe, Standing Bear and

122

President Calvin Coolidge wearing Sioux headdress presented to him in 1927, with the Indian title Wamblee-Tokaha, meaning Leading Eagle. (Photo by Rise, from *The Black Hills Engineer*, November 1927)

Chauncey Yellow Robe, in the costume he wore for the filming of the movie "The Silent Enemy" produced in New York, 1929. (Photo by Della B. Vlk)

Rosebud then conducted the President and Mrs. Coolidge back to their seats.

It was an important ceremony in more ways than one. It had been only a few short years since the tragedy at Wounded Knee, only a few more years since the Indian wars over the western prairies, the angry humbling of the Indian leaders and gathering of the tribes on the reservations. This was the hand of friendship offered from the Sioux leaders to the head of the United States, and President Coolidge took it in that way. His acceptance of the honor was symbolical of a new relationship between Indian and white.

John Coolidge arrived August 24, and thus was able to join the President and his First Lady when they visited the Pine Ridge Indian Reservation in the southern part of the state. Their itinerary took them first to the Niobrara Convocation of the Protestant Episcopal Church where several hundred Indians waited for them under the leadership of Bishop Burleson. Again the Sioux reiterated their wish for friendship and loyalty. Burleson read a declaration signed by three Sioux Christian ministers, which said in part:

". . . . We are the children and the grandchildren of those who fought on the Little Big Horn. It is the home of the last and the most stubborn of the fighting Sioux. A few miles to the east of you is Wounded Knee. Here your soldiers killed many of us. . . . . We repeat these facts to show the contrast between yesterday and today. Fifty years ago those who killed Custer hated the white man. Now in the same place are gathered hundreds of Christian Indians engaged in religious meetings.

. . . . No longer are the tomahawk and scalping knife stained with white blood, nor will they ever be again; in fact they no longer exist. . . . You have seen much of warpaint and feathers and dances. Those are all things of yesterday, which mean little today, and will mean nothing tomorrow. The hope of our people lies in education, industry, and religion, and we pray that you will help us find these necessities for a useful life. . . "[9]

In answering, the President gave the longest address that he had presented in his entire summer's stay in the Black Hills. As far as they were concerned, the Sioux had buried the hatchet for all time.

The visit of President Coolidge was important in two ways to the Yellow Robe family, changing their lives entirely. One of the newspapermen who covered the Coolidge activities was A. E. Seymour, New York. He took one look at the graceful beauty of Rosebud Yellow Robe and fell in love with her. They were married within a year or two, and Rosebud moved to New York with her husband.

Among the crowd witnessing the Sioux ceremony was somebody who recognized the personal magnetism of Chauncey Yellow Robe and the photographic quality which he possessed. In 1928 Chauncey was approached by the American Museum of Natural History

"to aid in the filming of a motion picture depicting American life on the continent before the advent of the white man."[10]

He resigned as Disciplinarian and went into Canada and Alaska for research and then filming of the movie. The proposed movie was filmed by a New York producer, the Burden Brothers, and was titled *The Silent Enemy*. Later, Mrs. Della B. Vik wrote:

"*The Silent Enemy* was the cold bitter winter with its great snow storms and the Indians huddled in their tepees with meager fires of faggots. They suffered hunger and sickness."[11]

Chauncey had been bitter about the movie in which the Wounded Knee massacre was portrayed in 1913, but this movie promised to show the Indians and their problems as they were. It was not surprising that he was offered the part. He had the classic profile of the red man in its greatest nobility. His lack of training as an actor could be easily corrected by good direction in the picture.

Mrs. Vik had good reason to remember that movie. Chauncey returned with the costume he was wearing as the star of the film, an authentic Sioux fringed shirt and buckskin pants, topped by the eagle feathered war bonnet of the Sioux chiefs. In that war bonnet, holding the ancient Sioux bow and arrows, Yellow Robe made a striking subject. Mrs. Vik's practiced eye caught his distinction immediately, and she persuaded him to let her make a series of portraits in the *Silent Enemy* costume.

Chauncey was at first dubious. An old Indian suspicion held that if a photo was torn or pierced, as he told Mrs. Vik,

"The original subject would die by a wound in the location marred."[12] We do not know whether the belief remains to this day or not, but it must have been fading somewhat in 1929 because Chauncey did reconsider and posed for the Vik photographs. Several of these outstanding photographs are published with this story, so unusual and striking that surely they speak for the entire Sioux nation.

He was in Rapid City only briefly, on the way back to New York to complete his work with the Museum and the movie. He had contracted a severe cold, but thought it was improving. It was not. In April the cold developed into pneumonia, and though he was hospitalized at the Rockefeller Institute Hospital, New York, he died April 6, 1930.

His body was shipped back to Rapid City for burial. With a Knights Templar escort, the funeral was held at the Masonic Temple in Rapid City and he was buried beside his wife in Mountain View Cemetery.

His daughter Rosebud was known throughout the Black Hills as one of the loveliest of Indian maidens. Mrs. Vik knew the Yellow Robe family, and with Chauncey's permission she photographed Rosebud many times for the sheer joy of creating beautiful pictures. Mrs. Vik wrote:

> "The oldest daughter, Rosebud, was married before Chauncey's death. She was exceptionally beautiful. I photographed her many times. Chauncey was always present even when I photographed her atop Hangman's Hill, and another pose of her down on her knees by Rapid Creek looking at her reflection in the water. Rosebud had all the full blood Sioux looks and in a very refined way. She was exceedingly graceful and naturally gracious."[13]

Chauncina, the second daughter, left South Dakota in 1929. Five years later she married Lee White Horse, an Arapahoe Indian, and the family lived in Chicago for many years. White Horse came from Oklahoma, so Chauncina's visits were more often to the White Horse relatives in Oklahoma than to South Dakota. Part of the reason for her long absence from South Dakota after her departure may have been the fact that her father died soon after she left Rapid City. As the years passed, Chauncina and Lee White Horse had two children, a son and a daughter. Both children were grown and married by the time Chauncina came back to the Black Hills, but the day came when she did return. She was asked to unveil the Chief Spotted Tail historical monument at Rosebud Indian Reservation in South Dakota in 1967. She was employed at the time by the R. H. Donnelly advertising agency in directory advertising sales, so was very much in touch with modern problems. In discussing the Spotted Tail monument, Chauncina remarked that such monuments of Indian leaders and Indian historical sites help American tourists to understand early American history and the Indian people. She advocated that Mount Rushmore, famed Shrine of Democracy in the Black Hills, should somehow manage to add a fifth face,

> "that of one of the Indian leaders who were equally as great to the first people in this country."[14]

The third daughter, Evelyn, was well educated. She was a child of eight when her father died, so went to New York to live with Rosebud. She was educated at Mount Holyoke College with her Masters and Ph.D. degrees at Northwestern University. A talented and gifted woman, she taught on the faculties of both Mount Holyoke and Vassar colleges. She recorded the Dakota language, and in 1954 received a Fulbright Award for the study of the physiology of the larynx at the Faculte de Medecine in Paris. She lectured at medical centers in several European cities, and then returned as Lecturer in Otolaryngology and Assistant Director of the Voice Clinic at Northwestern University Medical School.

Evelyn married Professor Hans Finkbeiner, M.D., and lives in Germany with her husband. Other honors bestowed upon her include the French Government award for excellence in French in 1940, and the Indian Council Fire Indian Achievement Award with an honorary life membership presented to her in 1946. She visited in the Black Hills in the 1940's or '50's, taking time to talk to her friend Mrs. Vik and another friend of many years, Nell Nielsen, both of Rapid City.

Though Chauncey Yellow Robe's obituary names only the three daughters as survivors, Clair F. Maynard, teacher at the Sioux Sanatorium Day School in

Rapid City, wrote that he knew Chauncey Yellow Robe, Jr. Mr. Maynard recalled:

> "I have seen their son, Chauncey Yellow Robe, paint Black Hills scenes, at which he was very good. When I came to Rapid City during the early '40's, he would be painting like at Gambles, and would complete such a picture in twenty to thirty minutes, selling them for $4.00. But I understand he moved to Arizona where he was engaged in religious work as a lay reader a few years ago."[15]

Red Cloud, Sitting Bull, Crazy Horse, Spotted Tail, Gall—all are the names of Indians known because of the times in which they lived, the last years of Sioux rebellion against the white men. Chauncey Yellow Robe knew the white man as a friend, he married a white woman, and he took part in the white man's civilization as an Indian leader of considerable renown. It is well to remember him and to know that the Indian people have men of such leadership and promise in their continuing life as American people.

In two generations, Chauncey Yellow Robe and his children traveled from the primitive culture of the prairie Indians to a plane of intelligence and culture considerably above the average American citizen of today. We in America can be proud of the Yellow Robe achievements.

References: Chauncey Yellow Robe, Bridge Between Two Cultures.

[1] Lee, Bob, "Sioux Spokesman Flays Cody and Miles over Indian War Film," *Rapid City Journal*, July 6, 1969. Rapid City, South Dakota.

[2] Yellow Robe, Chauncey, "Yellow Robe, Grand Nephew of Sitting Bull, Tells of His Boyhood Days with Sioux," *Rapid City Holiday Greetings*, 1915, published by Rapid City Daily Journal, Rapid City, South Dakota.

[3] Lee, Bob, opus cited.

[4] Lee, Bob, opus cited.

[5] Fielder, Mildred, "War Whoop!", *Rapid City Journal*, May 11, 1969. Rapid City, South Dakota.

[6] O'Harra, C. C., "President Coolidge in the Black Hills," *The Black Hills Engineer*, November 1927. South Dakota State School of Mines, Rapid City, South Dakota.

[7] O'Harra, opus cited.

[8] O'Harra, opus cited.

[9] O'Harra, opus cited.

[10] "Yellow Robe to be Buried Sunday," *Rapid City Daily Journal*, April 11, 1930. Rapid City, South Dakota.

[11] Vik, Della B., personal letter May 17, 1969.

[12] Vik, Della B., personal letter May 17, 1969.

[13] Vik, Della B., personal letter, May 17, 1969.

[14] "Sioux Honor Yellow Robe's Daughter," *Rapid City Journal*, 1967. Rapid City, South Dakota.

[15] Maynard, Clair F., personal letter September 29, 1971.

8.
BEN REIFEL, SIOUX CONGRESSMAN

The South Dakota prairie was hot with the wind. Young Ben Reifel patted the rough hide of a cow as it passed him to enter the barn. It was time for milking, the twilight hours of the day when the shadows were mixing with daylight and mosquitoes were humming in black clouds over the heads of the cattle.

One old cow bawled her low protest.

Ben said to one of his brothers, "They ought to have more grain, maybe."

"Why? They eat good as any cows."

"I think they would give more milk," said Ben. "But how can we get better feed for them? And what ought it to be?"

His brother gave a dry little laugh. "That's the trouble with you, Ben—you're always figuring different ways of doing things. Nothing's wrong with the old ways."

"I don't suppose," admitted Ben. "But why can't we make things better? And how do we do it?"

Those questions plagued Ben Reifel the rest of his life, drove him to school, to college, to graduate courses, and ultimately led him to almost the highest honor that America can give its young men — a seat in the United States Congress. He must find out what could be done to make life better for cows or humans, and he had to act on that knowledge.

He was born on a Sioux Indian reservation near Parmelee, Rosebud Reservation, South Dakota, September 19, 1906. His mother was a full blood Sioux, Lucy Burning Breast, and his father was a German-American, William Reifel, locally known as Shorty.

Their log cabin was tight against the weather, set on the small farm which William tilled with the help of his sons. Five boys were born to the couple, Ben, John, George, Alex and Albert. They had a few cows for milk and butter, horses to ride and to pull the farm plow or hay rake, a few chickens for eggs and an occasional chicken stew. The garden furnished vegetables. It was a good life for a growing boy, a good place to meet the summer's sun and the winter's cold and all the living wildlife of the prairie.

Ben spoke Sioux, as did the rest of the Brule Sioux on the Rosebud. To his Brule friends he was known as Wiyaka Wanjila, which translated to Lone Feather, but to his father he was young Ben. His mother spoke very little English. William Reifel understood Sioux, but communication was at times difficult for him on the reservation. Nevertheless Ben remembered that it was his mother who encouraged him to read the few books they could get and who urged him to go to school when he was old enough to do so. Times were changing, she told him. He must be ready for the new life, because the old ways of the Indian were being changed every day.

At age five he began his education at the Rosebud Agency Government day school, a small boy with a questioning mind. When he was six, his parents moved back on the farm. The neighbors built their own log school house and hired a teacher for $25 per month. Later the state built county public schools, but schooling seemed hard to acquire. He was sixteen before he was graduated from the eighth grade, and gives credit to his teacher Ethel Kraus, now of Cottage Grove, Oregon, for getting him through the seventh and eighth grades all in one year.

Always his mother encouraged him, but that driving in his own mind needed little prompting.

Ben Reifel, First District Congressman from South Dakota for ten years, 1961-1971.

Years later, he remembered those days of school and wondered why his Indian friends had not reacted as he did to the miracles of education. Mostly they took life easily and stayed in school only as they were forced to do so. Ben reached avidly for knowledge.

"I grew up on the reservation," he said, "speaking Sioux all the time. Why did not the other Indians respond as I did?"[1]

It puzzled him, but did not stop him. Perhaps one of the books which came into his hands influenced him, he said later. It was a western novel with a character in it named Whispering Smith. A rancher in that Whispering Smith book had a Master's Degree! Ben was a boy, and a Master's Degree sounded like something unattainable, something almost beyond reason, a dream perhaps.

He wanted more education, but the family had little money and Ben had only that eighth grade diploma. Then he learned that his Indian blood had advantages that he could use. In 1924 he became eighteen years old, thus a registered member of the Rosebud tribe. On reaching that majority, certain Sioux benefit money was his to use as he wanted. A Secondary South Dakota School of Agriculture existed in Brookings, South Dakota, which he could attend with that Sioux money backing him. By October 1925 he was in Brookings, studying.

In 1928 he had finished his secondary education to the extent that he was allowed to enroll as a special student in South Dakota State College at Brookings, majoring in chemistry and dairy science. He wanted to learn all he could about agricultural improvement. He could take the knowledge back to the reservation and hope it would help others.

During the summer of 1930 he worked in barberry eradication field work for the United States Department of Agriculture. He added ROTC military training to his schedule, and in 1931 was commissioned a Second Lieutenant in the United States Army. In his senior year he was elected president of the Students' Association, and graduated June 1932.

"After graduation I went to the Episcopal Hare School of Boys," Reifel remarked, "where I was given the opportunity to be Boys' Advisor for a year."[2]

Young, idealistic, fresh from college, his energies spilled over with enthusiasm. On July 1, 1933 he was given the position of Farm Agent at Pine Ridge Indian Reservation with headquarters at the little town of Oglala. This was the type of thing that he had wanted from the beginning. He was in a position to use his training in agricultural improvement, and he was delighted with the position. Six months later, December 26, 1933, he married a college classmate, Alice Janet Johnson, of Erwin, South Dakota.

Alice was a slightly built, light haired affectionate girl who was destined to be Ben's helpmate in many ways. She had been studying Home Economics in college.

"We hadn't been settled many months before I was asked to take a job in Pine Ridge," Alice wrote later. "WPA had set up a quilt making factory to employ the Indian women. They needed a Home Economist to supervise. I was the only one in the area so I began driving the fifteen miles from Oglala to Pine Ridge each day while Ben worked in the Oglala office."[3]

The William Reifel farm in 1927. Ben Reifel's saddle horse is in center of picture. The log cabin in which Ben was born is to the extreme left behind the windmill tower.

The Reifel family. Mr. and Mrs. William Reifel standing in center front. Their five sons, are left to right, Alex, Albert, George, Ben and John.

The WPA to which Alice Reifel referred was the Works Progress Administration, a government schedule of work to make jobs for those who could find work in no other way. Some called it boondoggling, but others knew it as the only possible salvation in sight.

It was 1934. South Dakota was in the depths of the drought years and the depression years. A quarter of a dollar looked like a cartwheel in those days. People lived on whatever they could get. Clothes were mended and made over to fit another child, never thrown away until they were thin as lace and as ragged. Food was precious, never wasted in the slightest way, and yet folks who knew those depression days lived through them and learned that they could handle any problem they might meet.

The Reifels were comfortable, though salaries were infinitesimal for everyone.

"Our little house had a water system," Alice wrote. "The water pumped by a windmill was forced into a storage tank in our attic. We did not have electricity. We used a gas stove, gas lamps, and we had a coal furnace. We had an old fashioned ice box which necessitated two trips a week to Pine Ridge Agency for ice."[4]

Ben remembered the opportunities for work that he had in those Pine Ridge days. Under Commissioner of Indian Affairs John Collier, the whole Indian program was being reorganized with cottage industries where feasible, and the quilt factory had been one of such industries. The Indian Reorganization Act of 1932 allowed the forming of business councils, a chance for Indians to plan their own way of living.

In 1935 the Reifels were transferred to Pierre, South Dakota, where Ben was assigned Organizational Field Agent for North and South Dakota, Nebraska, parts of Minnesota and Montana. Through the summer months Alice tried to stay with him during some of his travels, but with a baby due soon she went to stay with her parents in South Dakota.

Their daughter Loyce Nadine Reifel was born September 8, 1935 in a hospital at Watertown, South Dakota near her parents' home. Ben's work kept him traveling over the five state allocation which he tended, but he managed to be home long enough to meet his new daughter. She was a tiny baby, black haired, brown eyed, and according to her mother, "jaundiced,"[5] a condition which she outgrew speedily.

Alice and the baby were back in Pine Ridge long enough to pack for the final trip to Pierre. The day was November 11, 1935 when the Reifels moved their household goods from Pine Ridge to Pierre, a date remembered because they saw the stratosphere balloon pass over them as they drove over the prairie toward their new home.

The National Geographic Society had sponsored the stratosphere flights in the hope of new scientific information for humanity. The first had come down with a torn balloon, the second never got off the ground, but the third flight was wonderfully successful. No man had ever reached such rare heights before, but on that chilly 1935 day they did. Captain Albert W. Stevens, safe in his lofty gondola, made the first photograph ever to show the actual curvature of the earth. They reached 72,395 feet, the highest point ever reached by man to that day. In this year of the 1970's man has flown to the moon and back and has sent machines hurtling into the vast spaces beyond the moon, but in 1935 the stratosphere flight was a phenomenal achievement!

Ben was hard at work in his new assignment. The Wheeler Howard Act permitted Indians to organize in charters. In his capacity as Organization Field Agent Ben Reifel explained the law to the Indian tribes. They could vote for laws to apply to themselves. A tribal governing body could enact ordinances and judicial decisions. This was a step forward from the days when the first Indian police had been organized on Sioux Reservations. The Indian police had served

Ben was a freshman at South Dakota State College, Brookings, South Dakota, 1928.

Ben in his R.O.T.C. military uniform at South Dakota State College, Brookings, South Dakota, 1930.

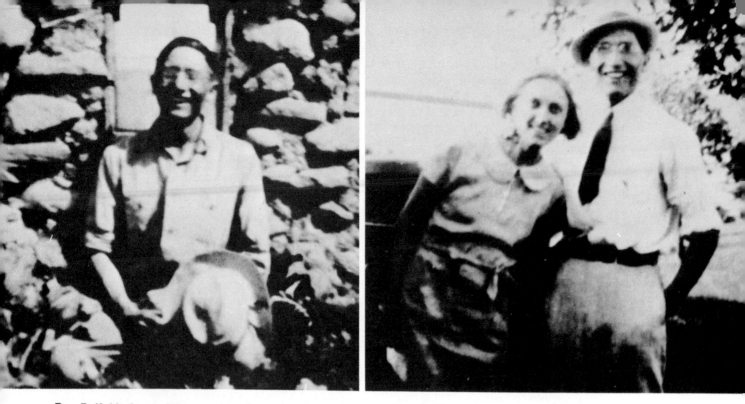

Ben Reifel in front of the remains of an old sod house, while on field work with the United States Department of Agriculture in barberry eradication in Edmunds County, South Dakota, summer of 1930.

Ben Reifel and Alice Johnson at Brookings, South Dakota, 1931, when they were college classmates there.

well, but white agents had directed them. By 1935 the Sioux were making their own decisions.

That winter of 1935-36 was a bitterly cold one. Alice laughed later, remembering, "An old Swedish man described it, 'Vun day the wind she blow the snow nort, the next day the vind she blew the snow sout!' "[6] but it was not funny then. The temperature was often twenty below zero during February, but Ben was home that month to help Alice.

She hated to have him gone so much, but the job kept him moving from state to state. Alice and baby Loyce traveled with Ben during the summer to keep the family together, but when winter returned it was necessary to settle in Pierre again.

"The spring that Loyce was eighteen months old," Alice wrote, "Ben had to go to the Pine Ridge area. Weather and roads were fine so Loyce and I went along. We decided to make a side trip to spend the night with dear friends in a remote little village. There had been considerable snow in that vicinity. A car had previously been stuck. We landed in the same tracks, badly mired with no way out. We were miles from anyone or any place. We made the decision to walk to our friends rather than sitting through the night in the car.

"We were not dressed for such a trip. It was fortunately a quiet, beautiful moonlight night. There was no road to follow. Snow had covered all tracks and trails . . . Ben knew the area well so he led the way carrying Loyce wrapped in an army blanket . . . I had trouble following Ben. I'd step into snow up to my hips. We did get to our destination after a six hour walk . . . That trip was a lesson for us. We never again went on any trip without plenty of extra clothes, blankets, food, etc."[7]

Perhaps because of the cold winters, Ben and Alice took a trip to Florida around 1939 to visit friends and to see the Everglades.

"Our trip into the Everglades in a swamp buggy was like going into another world,"[8] Alice remembered.

132

Ben Reifel when he was Extension Agent on the Pine Ridge Indian Reservation in 1933, posing with an Oglala friend, White Cow Bull. Reifel's Indian name was Wiyaka Wanjila, which translated to Lone Feather.

They returned to their work in the northern prairies, and in September 1941 Loyce began school. In Europe, Hitler was threatening to conquer the world. Winston Churchill was leading his Englishmen in resisting Hitler's armies, and the United States watched uneasily. Franklin Roosevelt, President of the United States, carried the news to the American people in his fireside talks, but there was little advance warning of the day when Pearl Harbor was attacked by Japanese warplanes on December 7, 1941.

America was at war.

Ben Reifel went to war as a Second Lieutenant, his first assignment at Leavenworth, Kansas with the Military Police. He says little about his war years other than that he was an MP in the states until just before the Japanese surrendered, at which time he was sent to Europe to France and Germany to help retrain soldiers for military police service there.

Alice and Loyce remembered different things about the war years. They meant to stay with Ben as long as they could do so and managed to join Ben at Leavenworth in June 1942. They moved to Fort Bliss, El Paso, Texas, with him, then Fort Smith, Arkansas, where Alice first learned about termites. They were at Camp Chaffee.

"Sundays, when Ben was on duty we were privileged to eat dinner with him at Camp Chaffee,"[9] Alice said.

Ben was sent to a special training school at Fort Custer, Michigan, then the family was able to join him at Dallas, Texas where they stayed for almost two years.

The Japanese surrendered August 14, 1945, but shortly before that day Ben had left for Europe. Alice and Loyce went to South Dakota, settling in Rapid City until Ben should return. Loyce became ill. To remain close to the Rapid City hospital where Loyce was being treated, Alice shared an apartment with a friend, Katherine Heacock, and remained there after Loyce's health began to improve. They were in Rapid City for a year. Ben returned to the states in April 1946 and was released from service the next month with the rank of Lieutenant Colonel in the Army Reserve. He was with his family by May 1946, but was suffering from an inner ear disturbance.

133

The Fort Berthold Indian Agency office located at Elbowoods, North Dakota when Ben Reifel was the superintendent was in the building at the right. Elbowoods (the town) and this area is now covered by the waters of Garrison Dam. (Photo by courtesy of Rev. H. W. Case)

Hoping to restore his health, the three Reifels took a trip through the south, west and back to the northern plains. By the middle of July he was ready to go to work again.

Ben Reifel began to be recognized as a man of promise.

His first appointment after the war was at the Regional Indian office at Billings, Montana, as Tribal Relations Officer, which he held from July 1946 to October 1946, a stopgap between his war years and his next important appointment, that of Superintendent at Fort Berthold, North Dakota. The Missouri River was in the process of being tamed, several huge dams being built along the length of the mighty river. The dams would furnish irrigation, hydroelectric power, soil conservation, and a series of inland lakes for recreational facilities such as boating, fishing, bird refuges and game development besides flood control.

The Garrison Dam was being constructed. It was necessary to get permission from the northern Indians to build on their land. Reifel talked to the Gros Ventres, the Mandans and Aricaras. For two years he negotiated between the Indians and the federal government.

"I was able to help work out a good settlement for the Indians,"[10] Reifel said, a trace of satisfaction in his voice. His loyalty lay with both his Indian friends and the United States Government, and it pleased him considerably that he was able to serve both in working with the Garrison Dam negotiations.

The family found a government house at Elbowoods, North Dakota, and once again were able to be together as Alice desired.

"It was evening as we drove toward our new home," she wrote. "Ben had traveled this territory in his work prior to World War II, but to Loyce and me it was new country. The graveled road wound round and up and down the hills which were dotted with prairie grass waving in the wind. The setting sun cast light and shadows all along the breaks, as the little hills are called that follow the wide Missouri River. How I had missed the gorgeous sunsets of the Dakotas! . . . We liked what we saw! . . ."[11]

Elbowoods was a tiny town, so small that we have never found it on any map. Fort Berthold has disappeared from today's maps, too, though you can find it on the older maps. Both were covered by Garrison Reservoir water when the dam was completed.

Elbowoods was mostly government buildings. An Agency office, Indian Boarding School buildings, government housing for teachers and other employees were there. Two stores operated on Main Street, and the post office was a corner in one of the stores. Two churches and some old mission buildings completed the business area.

Garrison Dam was forty miles downstream from the village of Elbowoods, and the land for the entire distance was owned by Aricara Indians. The Mandans and Gros Ventres lived upstream. Water in the Garrison Reservoir was expected to inundate the riverland for two hundred miles above the dam.

The Reifels found friends in the town from the beginning. Mrs. Wilde was an Aricara Indian who had been educated in Virginia and served on the Tribal Council. Mr. Wilde, also Aricara, had a degree in Agriculture from a North Dakota college. Both Mr. and Mrs. Wilde became good friends to the Reifels and were able to help Ben in his work with the three affiliated tribes, Aricara, Mandans and Gros Ventres.

Mrs. Helen Crowsheart was another Aricara woman of whom Alice was particularly fond. In many instances Alice spoke of the friendship offered by Helen. Perhaps the most touching token given by Helen Crowsheart was the Indian roach given by her to Superintendent Ben Reifel, a roach being a head decoration used for special ceremonials or dances. It was a treasured gift, an honor that both Ben and Alice appreciated.

For a while during 1948 the Reifels gave a home to a baby whose mother had died, a child whom they called Little Pete. They could not keep the baby boy with

A group of Mandans, Hidatsa and Arickaras at Fort Berthold Reservation who helped Ben Reifel in many ways during the negotiation for Indian lands for Garrison Dam, between 1946-1949. (Photo by courtesy of Rev. H. W. Case)

Three of the Mandan chiefs in ceremonial regalia at Fort Berthold Reservation, North Dakota, while Reifel was superintendent, 1946-1949. Left to right, Crowsheart, the oldest Mandan; Little Owl, Mandan; and Adelaide Stephenson, named after the grandfather of the politician. (Photo by courtesy of Rev. H. W. Case)

their schedule of work, so Little Pete went back to the hospital and then to relatives of his father's family.

Ben had been selected as a representative of the State Department in a group to tour parts of South America in 1947. While he was gone, Alice and Loyce visited her parents in South Dakota. The time would have been a pleasant one except for one thing. While he was in South America, Ben's mother Lucy Reifel died in a home fire.

"We could not get word to Ben," Alice said, "so Loyce and I joined Ben's four brothers and their families for the Sioux service in the Episcopal church at Parmelee, South Dakota. The saddened people of the community came to pay their respects to one of their loved and admired members."[12]

Ben returned to his work for Garrison Dam negotiations, but the problems were not easy. The Indians did not wish to leave their homelands and argued that the Army Engineers could find somewhere else for the dam. There was no other place. The Missouri River was where it was, and the dam must be built on the

136

river. Ben worked with the Tribal Council, and made many trips with them to Washington in their behalf. It took time. It took patience. Ben Reifel knew what both time and patience were, and used them during those years.

During the latter part of 1948 a government man was in Ben's office. He said, "Ben, Harvard University is offering a fine scholarship. Why don't you inquire about it?"[13]

Ben brushed the suggestion aside, but he thought about it enough that he mentioned it to Alice.

She said immediately, "Why don't you try for it? There's nothing to lose."[14]

"What would I do with the knowledge gained from a year at Harvard, and a Master's Degree?"[15]

His thoughts raced swiftly back to a year when he was a boy reading about Whispering Smith, and that rancher who had a Master's Degree. It was beyond his reach at that time, but—was it possible now? The idea intrigued him.

In 1949 he applied for the scholarship and won it. He had been awarded a scholarship in the Littauer School of Public Administration, and in September 1949 the family packed their bags and left for Harvard University and the historic town of Boston, Massachusetts.

The Reifel family found an apartment, entered Loyce in school, and settled to studying in earnest. Ben enrolled in as many credit courses as regulations allowed then signed for auditing additional classes. The privilege of studying at Harvard was an unexpected bonus, and he intended to make the most of it.

Garrison Dam on the Missouri River, North Dakota, 1973. This is one of the world's largest rolled fill dams, stretching 2 miles across the Missouri River Valley. More than 100 miles long, it boasts 1500 miles of shoreline. (Photo by courtesy of Rev. H. W. Case)

Map of County, Municipal, State and National Parks in North Dakota. The Garrison Dam on the Missouri River is prominent on the left center of map, with Fort Berthold Indian Reservation between two arms of the dam. Reifel worked between 1946 to 1949 as superintendent of the Fort Berthold Indian Reservation in arranging transfer of Indian lands to the Garrison Dam project. (Map by courtesy of Rev. H. W. Case)

He finished that first school year in 1950 with his Master's Degree in Public Administration, and qualified for a John Hay Whitney Fellowship for additional study. He spent most of his time in the social relations department at Harvard, with the old questions probing at his consciousness.

"I wanted to know why the Indians did not respond to advantages made available to them through churches, schools and so on," he said.

Thinking about the problem as he worked the three additional years at Harvard, he said, "I came to the conclusion that what you had was a question of two life styles. The Indians were a people who were oriented to the present whereas the North American whites were oriented to the future. The Indians lived in harmony with nature while the whites were dedicated to the conquering of it."[17]

The Sioux have no word for time, Reifel explained, nowhere in any Indian language could he find any such denotation. The whites believed in saving for the future, Indians did not. Perhaps the difference in their way of living through the past centuries made it impossible for Indians to save. The Indian hunters brought buffalo to camp and that meat must be eaten immediately by the entire tribe or dried for winter use. There was a difference in the attitude toward work between whites and Indians. The Indian men hunted for meat to bring it to their families. They fought to protect their wives and children from enemies, and necessarily the menial work was left for the women in camp. There was no other way to do it.

Reifel said that with the encroachment of whites on the Indian prairies the government leaders realized that they had to do something to help the Indian, and the Indian tribes became subject to the white way of living. The Indian buffalo economy was gone, he emphasized, and the Indian had to accept a new way of living.

Ben finished his residence requirements at Harvard in 1951 and received his Doctorate in 1952 with his thesis on Economics and Public Administration.

He was briefly in the Bureau of Indian Affairs Office in Washington, D. C., and then returned to Fort Berthold as Reservation Superintendent. He served in the same position for another year at the Pine Ridge Reservation in South Dakota, but in 1955 he was appointed Area Director of the Aberdeen Area Office, Aberdeen, South Dakota. It is of interest to know that Ben Reifel was the first Indian superintendent at Pine Ridge in its history. Pine Ridge Reservation was officially established in 1889 although it had functioned as the Red Cloud Agency for some dozen years before that.

As Area Director of Indian Affairs, Reifel's interests were varied. He became involved in the Boy Scout movement from the executive standpoint, several national service lodges, and community affairs. In August 1956 he was awarded the Outstanding American Indian Award at Sheridan, Wyoming, and at the same time was given the Indian Council Fire Achievement Award and honorary life

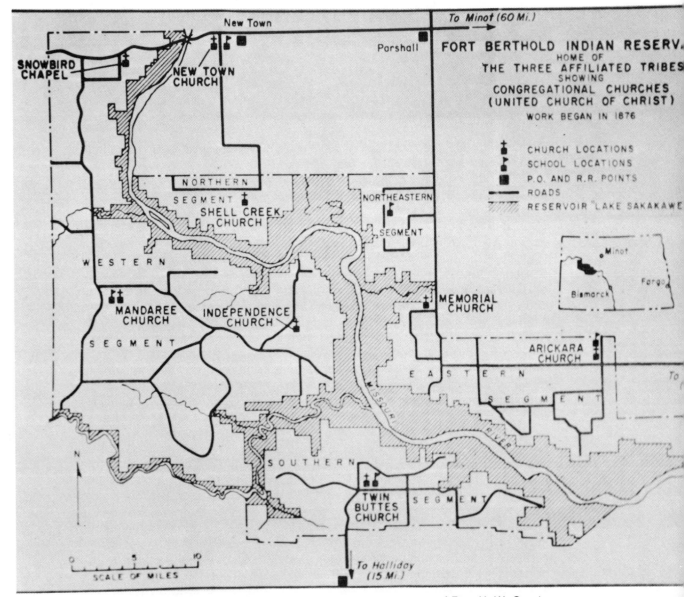

Fort Berthold Indian Reservation, 1973. (Map by courtesy of Rev. H. W. Case)

Ben Reifel with Scouters, left to right, Clayton Roseth, Aberdeen, South Dakota; Bob Gill, Aberdeen; Reifel; Dale Hieb, Ipswich, South Dakota; and Paul Gill, Aberdeen. Reifel worked on a national and state level with the Boy Scouts of America, and was awarded various honors for his work.

membership. He joined the Indian service organization called Arrow, Inc., and later was national president for that group.

He became a member of the Elks Lodge, the Masons, and Rotary. His military service led him to join the American Legion, the Veterans of Foreign Wars and Disabled American Veterans. He became a member-at-large of the National Council of the Boy Scouts of America, was a member of the Executive Committee, Region X, Boy Scouts of America, and served twice as president of the Pheasant Council of the Boy Scouts of South Dakota. In 1960 he was presented the Boy Scouts of America Silver Antelope Award.

When asked to help in the field of education, he served on the University of South Dakota Development Committee. He was also a member of the Upper Midwest Regional Educational Laboratory, which has since been disbanded. At present he is on the Board of Trustees for Huron College. He is first Vice President on the Board of Directors of the National Easter Seal Society.

When the suggestion was made to him that he could help even more by running for Congress, he decided to give it a try. March 11, 1960 he resigned his position with the Bureau of Indian Affairs and ran for Congress on the Republican ticket. He won easily, and moved to Washington to take part as First District Congressman from South Dakota in the 87th Congress. During that first session Reifel served on the House Agriculture Committee.

He was the first Sioux Indian, though he was only half Sioux by blood inheritance, to serve in the United States Congress in all the years since the first days of the republic.

"I wanted to repay, through public service, part of the debt I owe this republic,"[18] he said.

He was re-elected four more times to his Congressional seat, serving on the 88th, 89th, 90th, and 91st Congressional sessions. He was on the House Appropriations Committee, and served on the Interior, Related Agencies, and Legislative Subcommittees, and was the ranking minority member on the former.

When we asked him what he considered his most important work during those years, he reflected for a moment and then answered.

"I tried to make members of Congress become more aware of the needs of the Indians. While I was there, the appropriations from Congress for Indians went up rapidly, but this could be a part of the total ethnic situation. Interest is increasingly taken in all minorities now. I discussed the syndrome of the two life styles of the Indians and whites, and also tried to make Indians themselves aware that this is the problem.

"Education to make the Indians' future in the larger society is important. I was interested in trying to provide an education for all the children on the Reservation, and was able to get appropriations from Congress for Rosebud schools. Busses bring the Indian and white children near Mission (on the Rosebud Reservation) to school as part of the county school system now. The Sisseton schools are consolidating under a similar setup, one school for both reds and whites."[19]

He paused a moment, then added, "Indians must move forward. There will always be Indian problems in the back areas. Pine Ridge has about ten thousand people on it, about two thousand families. They stay because the reservation gives

Ben Reifel and family. Left to right, on couch, Loyce Anderson, Reifel, Valerie Anderson, Mrs. Reifel. Seated on floor, Laurie and Lisa Anderson.

Former President Dwight D. Eisenhower and Ben Reifel at the 87th Club Breakfast in Washington, D. C., June 12, 1963. Reifel began his duties as First District Congressman from South Dakota on the day when Eisenhower finished his terms as president.

Barry Goldwater with Ben Reifel. Goldwater ran for Republican candidate for President in 1964, while Reifel was South Dakota Congressman.

them more attention, free hospitals, schools, welfare, and so on, things that they cannot get off the reservation in towns."[20]

Though Ben and Alice had traveled abroad several times while he was in Congress, visiting Africa, Europe, South America and Asia, and he was well content with the progress he had made as South Dakota Representative to Congress, he voluntarily retired at the end of his fifth term January 2, 1971. He made no comment on his retirement, but it is apparent that the two of them wished to do some travel on a personal basis. He was offered the position of consultant and Special Assistant for Indian Programs to the Director of the National Park Service, United States Department of the Interior. He accepted the appointment without salary, since it meant some freedom of movement and a remaining close tie with the Indian people.

In May 1971 he was also appointed to the National Capital Planning Commission as chairman, a position which he was to hold for the next two years into 1973, also without salary. Obviously his retirement was not from public service as such, but only from his Congressional position from South Dakota.

The next month, June, his contribution to the nation was recognized when he received the honorary Doctor of Humanities from the South Dakota State University in which he had enrolled 43 years previously as a young Sioux with dreams of helping his Indian people and the nation, and an honorary degree of Doctor of Laws from the University of South Dakota in August.

Ben and Alice had a year together after his retirement. Loyce had married Emery Anderson in 1957 and with their three daughters, Lisa, Laurie, and Valerie joined Ben and Alice occasionally when they could.

"We traveled around America visiting national parks," Ben said, "such as Zion National Park, or the Bad Lands of South Dakota. We met Indian tribes in various sections to advise where National Park services could help them in developing their land. We traveled the country besides, part recreation, part business."[21]

He explained his work with the National Park Service as the opportunity to help Indians designate their land where it could be converted to advantage as parks, recreational areas or campgrounds as a means of increasing tribal income. The proposed Indian Cultural Parks are suggested by the National Park Service in an attempt to preserve Indian culture. The use of the Bad Lands National Monument in conjunction with the Oglala Sioux lands is an example.

Wherever he talked to Indians he made an effort to help them with their problems. It was an interesting year for both of them, but during the middle of the winter, February 8, 1972, Alice died suddenly of influenza-pneumonia at Walter Reed Hospital in Washington. She had a sore throat, and two days later she was gone. She had lived 62 years. Ben brought her body home to Aberdeen, South Dakota, where they had spent the last years of their work with the Indian Bureau. She was buried at Erwin, South Dakota, where her parents were also buried.

Reifel's immediate reaction was that he must work again at something which would demand his time completely. He announced that he would return to politics in the state of South Dakota. The newspapers were elated at the announcement, but as Ben talked to his constituents he began to realize that there might be problems in his return to political action.

"My desire to be of public service remains as strong today,"[22] he said in a press interview, referring to his original entry into public affairs, yet three weeks later he withdrew his announcement and turned his support to South Dakota's Attorney General Gordon Mydland.

The *Rapid City Journal*, editorializing, said:

"In the span of three weeks, former Congressman Ben Reifel sent up a test balloon and then promptly hauled it down with the declaration he would not be a candidate for the Republican United States Senate nomination. Reifel explained Tuesday the money needed to campaign had not materialized."[23]

Appropriation Committee session, Sub-committee on Interior and Related Agencies, 1964. Left to right: Representative from South Dakota Ben Reifel; Wyoming Representative William Henry Harrison; Chairman Mike Wirwan, Ohio; Committee Clerk Gene Wilhelm; and Mrs. Julia Hansen, Washington, D. C.

Committee discussing Oahe Irrigation Project on the Missouri River, February 1, 1966, at Washington, D. C. Left to right, seated: South Dakota Congressman E. Y. Berry; South Dakota Senator George McGovern; South Dakota Senator Karl Mundt; and Congressman Ben Reifel. Standing, Floyd Dominy and Ken Holum.

Ben Reifel, right, talking to South Dakota visitors at the Capitol in Washington, D. C., May 7, 1968. C. Peter Eggen, Sisseton, left. J. E. Krull, Watertown, center.

Ben and Alice Reifel campaigning for Ben's return to Congress, August 1968, Huron, South Dakota. (Photo by Mrs. F. F. Robinson, by courtesy of the Reifel family.

It may have been more than that. Personal reasons may have been matched by political pressures, and his age might have given him second thoughts when he had had time to reconsider.

Ben Reifel threw his support to the Republican ticket as he always had done, and continued his work with the National Parks Service.

When the completely renovated Jewel Cave facilities were dedicated in the Black Hills May 25, 1972, Ben Reifel was asked to be the Master of Ceremonies in a dedication which included several well known names. Retired Congressman E. Y. Berry, McLaughlin, South Dakota, was there. United States Representative James Abourezk, Rapid City, and National Park Service officer Howard Baker, Omaha, were on the stand. Dave Todd, park manager, was naturally part of the program as well, with Mr. and Mrs. Herb Conn, Custer, who had mapped much of the Jewel Cave trails. Other dignitaries present included other National Park officers and representatives of historical societies, state, county and city officials and state legislators.

Not long after that affair we met and talked to Ben Reifel in Rapid City, where he paused briefly before flying to Alaska on another National Parks mission. When we asked what the general opportunities for the Indian are today, he answered enthusiastically and immediately, "Great!"

He said the Indians' problem today is still cultural.

"Romanticists want to keep them the same as they were, but Indians have to accommodate to today. They want a modern standard of living the same as whites. They want TV sets, good cars, all the rest of it, in spite of the romanticists' notion of keeping the Indians as they were. The Indians cannot go back to the buffalo economy, and they know it."[25]

Even the Eskimos in Alaska, Reifel noted, have gone completely modern today wherever they can get the facilities, and full blood Eskimos are bankers, politicians, and so forth in Alaska towns.

144

Reifel's belief in the good life for the American Indian today is supported by statements given by several Indian leaders of today. Mrs. Eva J. Nichols, Rapid City, mentioned the many areas of business and community service open to the Indian people in a recent press interview:

> "We have in this community Indian teachers and school board members, Indian radio announcers, Indian businessmen, registered nurses, secretaries, dentists, lawyer, professional people in buildings and trades, health and welfare, and many other positions peculiar to this area . . . In spite of rumors, no Indian is forced to live on a reservation nor is he forced to live in any town. He can move about freely. He can always move if he feels he does not like a town or its people . . ."[26]

Carroll Swan, interviewed at the same time, echoed Mrs. Nichols' report:

> "Increased Indian involvement in Community Action Agency programs came in 1971 with leadership in such fields as day care, housing, job development, alcoholism programs and family planning . . . Native American involvement in local government is increasing with Art LaCroix on the city council, Harold Shunk re-elected to the school board over two other Indian candidates, Mrs. Muriel Waukazoo on the Democratic Central Committee and Carroll Swan on the Pennington County Democratic Advisory Committee . . ."[27]

Ben Reifel and President Richard M. Nixon, Washington, D. C. Reifel served under President Nixon for two years as First District Congressman from South Dakota between 1969 and 1971.

Ben Reifel and his daughter Loyce Anderson at the Anderson home in Delta, Colorado, 1969.

Mr. and Mrs. Ben Reifel and family visiting Mancos Canyon Ute Mountain Ute Reservation archeological areas in connection with National Park Service assistance to the Ute Mountain Ute Tribe in the development of an Indian Park, April 1971. Loyce Anderson is second from left, her husband Emery Anderson stands in the center. Their three daughters stand in front and left of them. Alice and Ben Reifel are at the right.

Raymond Becich, service unit director at the Rapid City Public Health Service Indian Hospital in 1972, was equally optimistic about the future of the American Indian in South Dakota:

> "I see the day approaching when Indians will entirely manage their own health problems, but it's going to take time to train Indian people and help make them aware of how to run their own health programs . . ."[28]

Indian Public Health Services, a federal agency, is increasing the number of Indians in the health field by training physicians' assistants and community health representatives, he noted.

Indian students have college scholarships available to them, and are increasingly taking advantage of such scholarships. Summer field programs are giving them opportunities for practical work experience as well.

An August press release announced the marriage of Ben Reifel August 21, 1972 to Frances Ryland Colby, in Durango, Colorado. Frances, her former husband Irvin Colby, Alice and Ben had been in college together at Brookings, and were lifelong friends. Ben and Frances planned to make their home in

146

Washington, D. C. Mrs. Colby's daughter, Mrs. John Honstad, and Ben Reifel's son-in-law, Emery Anderson, Durango, were attendants.

Ben's brothers carved good lives for themselves through the years. Albert is a medical doctor, and Director of the Veterans Administration Clinic in Henderson, Nevada. George was an educator and is now living in Albuquerque, New Mexico following his retirement. Alex is an engineer with the Corps of Engineers, Los Angeles. John was a carpenter at the Rosebud Boarding School and then maintenance engineer at the Pierre Indian School, but was killed in an auto accident in 1970.

Because of the dedicated services of Ben Reifel and others who have worked with him, the American Sioux Indian has come a long way since Lewis and Clark went up the Missouri River in 1804. The explorers found a non-literate people clothed in animal skins, eating fruits and roots and depending on buffalo for almost their complete sustenance, food, shelter, clothing. Today the Sioux are a part of modern living. They have bridged a civilization gap in less than two hundred years that took the white race over two thousand years to develop.

Race relations between red and white men have changed drastically since the day when Crazy Horse took a bayonet in his belly. Today the Indian and the white man work side by side, one as welcome as the other.

Red and white people have always intermarried. They still intermarry to the point where a full blood American Indian is hard to find, but every Sioux is proud of the Indian blood within him. A man on the Crow reservation said, "All the Indian blood in me would hardly fill one big toe," but he had Indian blood, and he boasted of it.

Ben Reifel, left, receiving the honorary degree of Doctor of Laws at the University of South Dakota, Vermillion, South Dakota, 1971. With him, right, is Dr. Richard Bowen, president of the University.

Left to right, Dr. Hilton Briggs, President of South Dakota State College, Brookings, South Dakota; Miss Geraldine Fenn, and Ben Reifel. Miss Fenn and Reifel were awarded honorary Doctor of Humanities degrees from South Dakota State College, 1971.

Ben Reifel was master of ceremonies at the dedication of the Jewel Cave Visitor Center, Black Hills, South Dakota, May 28, 1972.

The lifetime of service that Ben Reifel gave to his country and to his Sioux compatriots is part of a new day in America. That we have such men as Ben Reifel is the salvation of our land, and the promise of the future.

Quotation References: Ben Reifel, Sioux Congressman

[1] Ben Reifel, interview 1972.
[2] Reifel interview.
[3] Reifel, Mrs. Ben (Alice), unpublished manuscript, p. 26.
[4] Alice Reifel, p. 26
[5] Alice Reifel, p. 28
[6] Alice Reifel, p. 29
[7] Alice Reifel, p. 29, 30
[8] Alice Reifel, p. 31
[9] Alice Reifel, p. 35
[10] Ben Reifel, interview
[11] Alice Reifel, p. 3 Post War
[12] Alice Reifel, p. 15 Post War
[13] Alice Reifel, p. 16 Post War
[14] Alice Reifel, p. 16 Post War
[15] Alice Reifel, p. 16 Post War
[16] Ben Reifel, interview
[17] Ben Reifel, interview
[18] "Reifel Available as Candidate," *Rapid City Journal*, February 25, 1972. Rapid City, South Dakota.
[19] Ben Reifel, interview
[20] Ben Reifel, interview
[21] Ben Reifel, interview
[22] "Reifel Available as Candidate," *Rapid City Journal*, February 25, 1972. Rapid City, South Dakota.
[23] "Reifel's Decision and What Lies Ahead for the Republican Party," *Rapid City Journal*, March 23, 1972. Rapid City, South Dakota.
[24] Ben Reifel, interview
[25] Ben Reifel, interview
[26] Nichols, Mrs. Eva J., "The Urban Indian: The Conservative's View," *Rapid City Journal*, February 20, 1972. Rapid City, South Dakota.
[27] Swan, Carroll, "The Urban Indian: The Activist's View," *Rapid City Journal*, February 20, 1972. Rapid City, South Dakota.
[28] Higgins, Harold, "Sioux San Director Sees Day When Indians Will Take Over Programs," *Rapid City Journal*, July 23, 1972. Rapid City, South Dakota.

SIOUX INDIAN LEADERS

by Mildred Fielder

Bibliography: CRAZY HORSE

Anderson, Harry H., "A History of Cheyenne River Indian Agency and its Military Post, Fort Bennett, 1868-1891," *South Dakota Historical Collections, Volume XXVIII*. Pierre, South Dakota, 1956.

"Another Look at Custer's Last Stand," *Hersey-Sparling Metrogram*, El Monte, California, March 1970.

"Battle of Little Big Horn; Custer's Death Confirmed; His Command Wiped Out," reprint from *Black Hills Pioneer Times*, 1876, Deadwood, South Dakota.

Cannon, Jack, "Is Crazy Horse Crazy?" *Rapid City Journal*, June 14, 1959. Rapid City, South Dakota.

"Chicago Writer Discusses Last Stand of Custer," *Rapid City Daily Journal*, July 6, 1936. Rapid City, South Dakota.

"Continued Publicity Important to Crazy Horse Project," *Rapid City Journal*, February 21, 1971. Rapid City, South Dakota.

"Crazy Horse," *Black Hills Pioneer Times* reprint 1876. Deadwood, South Dakota.

DuBois, Charles G., "Battle of Little Big Horn Fought 91 Years Ago," *Rapid City Journal*, June 25, 1967. Rapid City, South Dakota.

Encyclopedia Americana, Americana Corporation, New York, 1965.
    Volume 8, Crazy Horse, p. 168.
    Volume 11, William Judd Fetterman, p. 158.
    Volume 11, Fort Phil Kearny, p. 514a.

Gladstone, Lyn, "Ziolkowski's Wife is Dedicated to Helping Him Carve Mountain," *Rapid City Journal*, March 30, 1967. Rapid City, South Dakota.

Herman, Eddie, "Betrayer of Crazy Horse Disgraced," *Rapid City Daily Journal*, December 10, 1950. Rapid City, South Dakota.

Herman, Eddie, "Noted Oglala Medicine Man Kept Crazy Horse's Secret," *Rapid City Daily Journal*, February 11, 1951. Rapid City, South Dakota.

Kingsbury, George W., *History of Dakota Territory*, ed. by George Martin Smith. The S. J. Clarke Publishing Company, Chicago, 1915. Volume I.

"Indian Treaty," *Black Hills Pioneer Times* 1876 reprint. Deadwood, South Dakota.

Koller, Joe, "New York Man Creates a New Bust of Crazy Horse," *Rapid City Daily Journal*, February 10, 1957. Rapid City, South Dakota.

Lee, Bob, "Ridin' the Range," *Rapid City Daily Journal*, July 29, year ?. Rapid City, South Dakota.

Lewis, Emily H., "Change from Bow Tie and Tails to Moccasins and Feathers Not Hard," *Rapid City Daily Journal*, January 19, 1958. Rapid City, South Dakota.

Lewis, Emily H., "Sioux Indians Believed in Seeing America First," *Rapid City Daily Journal*, August 30, 1959. Rapid City, South Dakota.

Luce, Edward S. and Evelyn S., *Custer Battlefield*, National Park Service, Washington, D.C. 1961.

Meadowcroft, Enid LaMonte, *The Story of Crazy Horse*, Grosset & Dunlap, New York, New York, 1954.

Mattison, Ray H., "Report on Historic Sites in the Oahe Reservoir, Missouri River," *South Dakota Historical Collections*, Volume XXVII. Pierre, South Dakota, 1954.

McDermott, Louis M., "The Primary Role of the Military on the Dakota Frontier," *South Dakota History*, Winter 1971. Pierre, South Dakota.

McGillycuddy, Julia B., *McGillycuddy: Agent.* Stanford University Press, Stanford, California 1941.

Robinson, Will G., "Digest of the Reports of the U.S. Indian Commissioner, 1853 to 1868." South Dakota Historical Collections, Volume XXVII and Volume XXVIII. Pierre, South Dakota 1954 and 1956.

Sandoz, Mari, *Crazy Horse, the Strange Man of the Oglalas.* Alfred A. Knopf, New York, New York, 1942.

Veglahn, Nancy, *The Buffalo King.* Charles Scribner's Sons, New York 1971.

Windolph, Charles, unpublished report of his part in the Battle of the Little Big Horn.

Bibliography: SPOTTED TAIL, THE STRATEGIST

"Crazy Horse," reprint from *Black Hills Pioneer Times*, June 8, 1876, Deadwood, Dakota Territory.

Hyde, George E., *Spotted Tail's Folk, a History of the Brule Sioux.* University of Oklahoma Press, Norman, Oklahoma, 1961.

"Indian Treaty," reprint from *Black Hills Pioneer Times*, June 8, 1876. Deadwood, Dakota Territory.

Jordan, William Red Cloud, "Eighty Years on the Rosebud," ed. Henry W. Hamilton, *South Dakota Department of History, Report and Historical Collections*, South Dakota State Historical Society, Volume XXXV, Pierre, South Dakota, 1970.

Kingsbury, George W., *History of Dakota Territory.* The S. J. Clarke Publishing Company, Chicago, 1915. Volume I.

Leedy, Carl, *Black Hills Pioneer Stories*, ed. by Mildred Fielder. Bonanza Trails Publishers, Lead, South Dakota 1972.

Mattison, Ray H., "Report on Historical Aspects of the Oahe Reservoir Area, Missouri River, South and North Dakota." *South Dakota Historical Collections and Report*, Volume XXVII, 1954. South Dakota Historical Society, Pierre, South Dakota 1954.

McDermott, Louis M., "The Primary Role of the Military on the Dakota Frontier," *South Dakota History*, Vol. 2, No. 1, Winter 1971. South Dakota State Historical Society Quarterly, ed. Dayton W. Canaday, Pierre, South Dakota, 1971.

McGillycuddy, Julia B., *McGillycuddy: Agent.* Stanford University Press, Stanford, California 1941.

Sandoz, Mari, *Crazy Horse, the Strange Man of the Oglalas.* Alfred A. Knopf, New York, N. Y. 1942.

"Sioux Honor Yellow Robe's Daughter," *Rapid City Daily Journal*, 1967. Rapid City, South Dakota.

Bibliography: SITTING BULL

"Aged Indian Woman Recalls Why Dad Shot Sitting Bull," *Rapid City Daily Journal*, April 12, 1953. Rapid City, South Dakota.

Anderson, Harry H., "A History of the Cheyenne River Indian Agency and its Military Post, Fort Bennett, 1868-1891," *South Dakota Report and Historical Collections*, Volume XXVIII. South Dakota Historical Society, Pierre, South Dakota, 1956.

"Crazy Horse," reprint from *Black Hills Pioneer Times*, June 8, 1876. Deadwood, South Dakota.

Cronau, Dr. Rudolf, "My Visit Among the Hostile Dakota Indians and How They Became My Friends," *South Dakota Historical Collections*, Volume XXII. South Dakota State Historical Society, Pierre, South Dakota, 1946.

Dancker, Dorothy, "Sitting Bull Still Controversial Figure 75 Years After His Death," *Rapid City Journal*, December 14, 1965. Rapid City, South Dakota.

Kingsbury, George W., *History of Dakota Territory*. The S. J. Clarke Publishing Company, Chicago, 1915. Volume I.

Koller, Joe, "Christmas 1890 Wasn't Very Gay; Hills Residents Feared Sioux War," *Rapid City Daily Journal*, December 24, 1950. Rapid City, South Dakota.

"Let the Young Men Rule Was Plea of Sioux Chief," *Rapid City Journal*, September 28, 1969. Rapid City, South Dakota.

Lewis, Emily, H., "Sioux Indians Believed in Seeing America First," *Rapid City Daily Journal*, August 30, 1959. Rapid City, South Dakota.

Luce, Edward S. and Evelyn S., *Custer Battlefield, National Monument, Montana*. National Park Service, Washington, D.C. 1949.

Mattison, Ray H., "Report on Historical Aspects of the Oahe Reservoir Area, Missouri River, South and North Dakota," *South Dakota Historical Collections and Report*, Volume XXVII. South Dakota State Historical Society, Pierre, South Dakota 1954.

McDermott, Louis M., "The Primary Role of the Military on the Dakota Frontier," *South Dakota History*, Vol. 2, No. 1, Winter 1971, South Dakota Historical Society Quarterly, Pierre, South Dakota, 1971.

McGillycuddy, Julia B., *McGillycuddy: Agent*, Stanford University Press, Stanford, California, 1941.

"The Murdering Cheyenne Indians," *Black Hills Pioneer Times* reprint from June 8, 1876. Deadwood, South Dakota.

Pett, Saul, "Two Sitting Bulls Ought to be Enough for Dakotas," United Press, date?

"Two Sitting Bulls; One Was Peacemaker, Other Was War Chief," *Rapid City Daily Journal*, February 28, 1954. Rapid City, South Dakota.

Poznansky, Lucille M., "Chief Sitting Bull, Sioux Patriot?" *Rapid City Daily Journal*, April 5, 1953. Rapid City, South Dakota.

Sandoz, Mari, *Crazy Horse, the Strange Man of the Oglalas*, Alfred A. Knopf, New York, N. Y., 1942.

"Sitting Bull," *Encyclopedia Americana*, Volume 25. Americana Corporation, New York, 1965.

"Sitting Bull is Fatally Wounded," *Black Hills Pioneer Times* reprint, from June 8, 1876. Deadwood, South Dakota.

Wetmore, Helen Cody, *Last of the Great Scouts*. University of Nebraska Press, Lincoln, Nebraska, 1966.

Windolph, Charles, unpublished letter.

Bibliography: GALL, RENO'S OPPONENT

"Battle of Little Big Horn, Custer's Death Confirmed; His Command Wiped Out," reprint from *Black Hills Pioneer Times,* 1876. Deadwood, South Dakota.

"Chicago Writer Discusses Last Stand of Custer," *Rapid City Daily Journal,* July 6, 1936. Rapid City, South Dakota.

DuBois, Charles G., "The Edgerly Narrative, 91 Years Ago Battle of Little Big Horn Fought," *Rapid City Journal,* June 25, 1967. Rapid City, South Dakota.

"Gall," *Encyclopedia Americana,* Volume 12. The Americana Corporation, New York, 1965.

"Gall's Oratory Impressed Country," *Rapid City Daily Journal,* Rapid City,

Kingsbury, George W., *History of Dakota Territory.* The S. J. Clarke Publishing Company, 1915. Chicago, Illinois.

Korn, Gustave, "The Custer Massacre," hand written copy of manuscript, writing believed to be that of John S. McClintock.

Lee, Bob, "Clearing of Reno Recalls Fort Meade Court Martial," *Rapid City Journal,* June 4, 1967. Rapid City, South Dakota.

Luce, Edward S. and Evelyn S., *Custer Battlefield, National Monument, Montana,* National Park Service, Washington, D.C. 1961.

Marshall, Brig. Gen. (Ret.) S.L.A., "Custer Committed a Series of Blunders," *Rapid City Journal,* March 14, 1971. Rapid City, South Dakota.

McGillycuddy, Julia B., *McGillycuddy, Agent.* Stanford University Press, Stanford, California 1941.

Poznansky, Lucille M., "Battle of Little Big Horn, Most Stirring Western Epic," *Rapid City Daily Journal,* June 28, 1953. Rapid City, South Dakota.

Sandoz, Mari, *Crazy Horse, the Strange Man of the Oglalas.* Alfred A. Knopf, New York, N. Y., 1942.

Windolph, Charles, typed statement given by Windolph to S. Goodale Price in the 1930's, published by S. Goodale Price, *Saga of the Hills,* Cosmo Press, Hollywood, Calif., 1940.

Utley, Robert M., *Custer Battlefield.* National Park Service, U.S. Department of the Interior, Washington, D.C., 1969.

Bibliography: MARTIN CHARGER, AND THE SHETAK CAPTIVES.

Anderson, Harry H., "A History of the Cheyenne River Indian Agency and its Military Post, Fort Bennett, 1868-1891." *South Dakota History Collections,* Vol. XXVIII, 1956. pp. 407-409. South Dakota Historical Society, Pierre, South Dakota.

Anderson, Harry H., letters July 11, 1961 and February 1, 1962.

Charger, Samuel, "Biography of Martin Charger," *South Dakota History Collections,* Vol. XXII, 1946. pp. 1-25. South Dakota Historical Society, Pierre, South Dakota.

Kingsbury, George W., *History of Dakota Territory.* The S. J. Clarke Publishing Company, Chicago, 1915.

Mattison, Ray H., "Report on Historical Aspects of the Oahe Reservoir Area, Missouri River, South and North Dakota, *South Dakota History Collections,* Vol. XXVII, 1954. South Dakota Historical Society, Pierre, South Dakota, 1954.

Morken, Cal, "Monument to Indian Chivalry Near Mobridge Becomes Migratory Marker," *Aberdeen American News,* Aberdeen, South Dakota.

Pattee, John, "Reminiscences of John Pattee," edited by Doane Robinson. *South Dakota History Collections,* Vol. V, 1910. South Dakota Historical Society, Pierre, South Dakota, 1910.

Robinson, Doane, editor, *South Dakota History Collections,* Vol V. 1910, p. 12, p. 350. South Dakota Historical Society, Pierre, South Dakota, 1910.

Skaug, Julius, *The Mobridge Murals, Mobridge Municipal Auditorium,* The Mobridge Reminder, Mobridge, South Dakota, undated.

"Big Foot's Band Pushed to Limits of Endurance," *Rapid City Journal*, 1963. Rapid City, South Dakota.

"Big Foot's Flight From Pedro Led to Massacre," *Rapid City Journal*, 1963. Rapid City, South Dakota.

Dibble, Redford, H., *"McGillycuddy: Agent* is Faithful Tale of a Great Indian Agent," *Rapid City Daily Journal*, March 26, 1941. Rapid City, South Dakota.

"Digest of Indian Commissioner Reports," *South Dakota Historical Collections*, Volume XXVI, 1952; Volume XXVII, 1954; Volume XXVIII, 1956. South Dakota Historical Society, Pierre, South Dakota.

"Fetterman, William Judd," *Encyclopedia Americana*, Volume 11. Americana Corporation, New York, 1965.

"Fort Phil Kearny," *Encyclopedia Americana*, Volume 11. American Corporation, New York, 1965.

"Indian Reservations in the United States," *Encyclopedia Americana*, Volume 15. Americana Corporation, New York, 1965.

"Indians on the Redwater," *Black Hills Pioneer Times* reprint from 1876 issues. Deadwood, South Dakota.

Kingsbury, George W., *History of Dakota Territory*, Volume I. The S. J. Clarke Publishing Company, Chicago, Illinois, 1915.

Koller, Joe, "Christmas 1890 Wasn't Very Gay; Hills Residents Feared Sioux War," *Rapid City Daily Journal*, December 24, 1950. Rapid City, South Dakota.

Koller, Joe, "Spotted Tail, Sioux Peacemaker, Termed Benefactor of Two Races," *Rapid City Daily Journal*, Rapid City, South Dakota.

Lee, Bob, "Ridin' the Range," *Rapid City Journal*, July 29. Rapid City, South Dakota.

"Let the Young Men Rule Was Plea of Sioux Chief," *Rapid City Journal*, September 28, 1969, Rapid City, South Dakota.

Lewis, Emily H., "Sioux Indians Believed in Seeing America First," *Rapid City Daily Journal*, August 30, 1959. Rapid City, South Dakota.

McDermott, Louis M., "The Primary Role of the Military on the Dakota Frontier," *South Dakota History*, Winter 1971, Volume 2., No. 1. South Dakota State Historical Society, Pierre, South Dakota, 1971.

McGillycuddy, Julia B., *McGillycuddy: Agent*. Stanford University Press, Stanford, California 1941.

Olson, James C., *Red Cloud and the Sioux Problem*. University of Nebraska Press, Lincoln, Nebraska, 1965.

"Red Cloud," *Encyclopedia Americana*, Volume 23. Americana Corporation, New York, 1965.

"Red Cloud's Band," *Black Hills Pioneer Times* reprint from 1876 issues. Deadwood, South Dakota.

Sandoz, Mari, *Crazy Horse, the Strange Man of the Oglalas*, Alfred A. Knopf, New York, N. Y. 1942.

Spindler, Will, "Only Early Pioneer Whites Saw Sioux Indian Buffalo Dance," *Rapid City Daily Journal*, January 25, 1953. Rapid City, South Dakota.

"Wounded Knee: A Black Day for Humanity," *Rapid City Journal*, December 27, 1970.

"Wounded Knee Battle Left 300 Sioux Dead," *Rapid City Journal*, 1963. Rapid City, South Dakota.

Bibliography: CHAUNCEY YELLOW ROBE, Bridge Between Two Cultures.

"Big Foot's Band Pushed to Limits of Endurance," *Rapid City Journal*, 1963. Rapid City, South Dakota.

"Big Foot's Flight From Pedro Led to Massacre," *Rapid City Journal*, 1963. Rapid City, South Dakota.

"Chronicle of President Coolidge's Summer in the Black Hills," *The Black Hills Engineer*, November 1927. South Dakota State Schools of Mines, Rapid City, South Dakota.

"Crowds Gather for Yellow Robe Funeral," *Rapid City Daily Journal*, April 14, 1930. Rapid City, South Dakota.

Gladstone, Lyn, "Continuing Tragedy," *Rapid City Journal*, December 27, 1970. Rapid City, South Dakota.

Gridley, Marion E., ed., *Indians of Today*, 4th edition, 1971. I.C.F.P. Inc.

Houck, George, map, *Vanishing Trail Expedition* 1963, Chamber of Commerce, Wall, South Dakota.

Hyde, George E., "What the Sioux Did to the Good Old Second Infantry," *Rapid City Daily Journal*, February 21, 1960. Rapid City, South Dakota.

"Indian Reservations in the United States," *Encyclopedia Americana*, Volume 15. The Americana Corporation, New York, 1965.

Koller, Joe, "Christmas, 1890, Wasn't Very Gay; Hills Residents Feared Sioux War," *Rapid City Journal*, December 24, 1950. Rapid City, South Dakota.

Koller, Joe, "Messiah Uprising Ended in Sioux Disaster," *Rapid City Daily Journal*, Rapid City, South Dakota.

Lambert, John T., "The Presidential News Service," *The Black Hills Engineer*, November 1927. South Dakota State School of Mines, Rapid City, South Dakota.

Lee, Bob, "Ridin' the Range," *Rapid City Daily Journal*, March 7, 1954, March 21, 1954, May 2, 1954. Rapid City, South Dakota.

Lee, Bob, "Sioux Spokesman Flays Cody and Miles over Indian War Film," *Rapid City Journal*, July 6, 1969. Rapid City, South Dakota.

Maynard, Clair, "Evelyn Yellow Robe (Dakota-Brule) University Lecturer," *Indians of Today*, ed. by Marion E. Gridley, 1971, 4th edition. I.C.F.P. Inc.

Maynard, Clair F., personal letter September 29, 1971, Rapid City, South Dakota.

Newport, K. K., personal letter October 25, 1971, Rapid City, South Dakota.

Nielsen, Nell, personal letter October 6, 1971, Rapid City, South Dakota.

O'Harra, C. C., "President Coolidge in the Black Hills," *The Black Hills Engineer*, November 1927. South Dakota State School of Mines, Rapid City, South Dakota.

"Sioux Honor Yellow Robe's Daughter," *Rapid City Journal*, 1967. Rapid City, South Dakota.

Stanley, John A., "Preparing the Presidential Home in the State Park," *The Black Hills Engineer*, November 1927. South Dakota State School of Mines, Rapid City, South Dakota.

"Vanishing Trails," Chamber of Commerce, Wall, South Dakota, 1963.

Vik, Della B., personal letters, May 17, 1969; September 21, 1971, September 25, 1971, interview 1968. Rapid City, South Dakota.

"Wounded Knee: A Black Day for Humanity," *Rapid City Journal*, December 27, 1970, Rapid City, South Dakota.

"Wounded Knee Battle Left 300 Sioux Dead," *Rapid City Journal* 1963, Rapid City, South Dakota.

Yellow Robe, Chauncey, "Yellow Robe, Grand Nephew of Sitting Bull, Tells of His Boyhood Days with Sioux," *Rapid City Holiday Greetings*, 1915, published by Rapid City Daily Journal, Rapid City, South Dakota.

"Yellow Robe to be Buried Here," *Rapid City Daily Journal*, April 10, 1930. Rapid City, South Dakota.

"Yellow Robe to be Buried Sunday," *Rapid City Daily Journal*, April 11, 1930. Rapid City, South Dakota.

Bibliography: BEN REIFEL, SIOUX CONGRESSMAN

Biography of Representative Ben Reifel, issued by the Office of Indian Programs, June 5, 1972 and 1970.

Corbett, Dr. Cecil, "Bridging the Cultural Gap," *Rapid City Journal*, June 13, 1971. Rapid City, South Dakota.

Fredrickson, Mary, "Jewel Cave Dedication Draws Many Dignitaries," *Lead Daily Call*, May 30, 1972. Lead, South Dakota.

Gridley, Marion E., ed. *Indians of Today*, 4th edition, 1971. I.C.F.P. Inc.

Higgins, Harold, "Sioux San Director Sees Day When Indians Will Take Over Programs," *Rapid City Journal*, July 23, 1972. Rapid City, South Dakota.

"Indian Collegians Learning in Summer Field Program at Mission Center," *Rapid City Journal*, August 27, 1972. Rapid City, South Dakota.

"Jewel Cave Dedication," *Lead Daily Call*, May 25, 1972. Lead, South Dakota.

"Mrs. Reifel Dies at 62 in Washington," *Rapid City Journal*, February 8, 1972. Rapid City, South Dakota.

"Mrs. Ben Reifel Dies in Capitol," *Lead Daily Call*, February 8, 1972. Lead, South Dakota.

Nichols, Mrs. Eva J., "The Urban Indian: The Conservative's View," *Rapid City Journal*, February 20, 1972. Rapid City, South Dakota.

"North Dakota," *Encyclopedia Americana*, Volume 20. The Americana Corporation, New York, 1965.

Reifel, Alice, unpublished autobiography.

"Reifel Available as Candidate," AP, *Rapid City Journal*, February 25, 1972. Rapid City, South Dakota.

Reifel, Ben, interview May 28, 1972.

"Reifel May Return to Politics in State," UPI, *Lead Daily Call*, February 25, 1972. Lead, South Dakota.

"Reifel, Mrs. Colby Wed in Colorado," AP, *Rapid City Journal*, August 23, 1972.

"Reifel's Decision and What Lies Ahead for the Republican Party," *Rapid City Journal*, March 23, 1972. Rapid City, South Dakota.

"Reifel Will Try for Senate," *Rapid City Journal*, March 9, 1972. Rapid City, South Dakota.

"South Dakota," *Encyclopedia Americana*, Volume 25. The Americana Corporation, New York, 1965.

Swan, Carroll, "The Urban Indian: The Activist's View," *Rapid City Journal*, February 20, 1972. Rapid City, South Dakota.

INDEX

Aberdeen, South Dakota—140, 143
Abourezk, James—144
Alaska—124, 144
Albany, New York—116
Albuquerque, New Mexico—147
Alexis, Grand Duke—29, 30
Allotment Act—83
American Fur Company—72, 76
American Horse—13, 23, 92, 95, 105, 106, 111
American Legion—140
American Museum of Natural History—124
Anderson, Emery—142, 146, 147
Anderson, Laurie—141, 142, 146
Anderson, Lisa—141, 142, 146
Anderson, Loyce—141, 142, 145, 146
Anderson, Valerie—141, 142, 146
Angry Eyes—76
Appropriation Committee—143
Arapahoes—27, 64, 90, 95, 106, 125
Aricaras—46, 72, 74, 90, 134, 135
Arizona—126
Arkansas—133
Army Reserve—133
Arrow, Inc.—140
Artichoke Eaters—74
Assiniboines—90

Bad Faces—13
Bad Lands—52, 53, 55, 111, 142
Bad Lands National Monument—143
Bad River—80, 84
Baker, Howard—144
Battle of the Little Big Horn—17, 19, 27, 31, 44-46, 60-62, 64, 68, 82, 104, 106, 110, 112, 119, 121
Battle of Platte Bridge—13
Battle of the Rosebud—16
Battle of Slim Buttes—20, 105
Battle of Washita—47
The Bear—91
Bear Ribs—74, 75
Berke, Ernest—21, 24
Beaver Creek—29
Becich, Raymond—146
Benteen, Captain Frederick W.—18, 19, 46, 60, 61, 62, 65
Bell, Captain James M.—110
Berry, E. Y.—143, 144
Big Bellies—13, 14
Big Crow—74
Big Foot—20, 53, 54, 55, 83, 111, 115
Big Horn Mountains—19, 40, 49, 61, 64, 97, 104
Big Leggins—21
Big Mouth—97
Big Road—17, 45
Billings, Montana—134
Bismarck, N.D.—51
Black Buffalo Woman—13, 14, 22
Black Crow—35
Blackfeet—26, 46, 82, 95, 105
Black Fox—20
Black Hills—11, 15, 20, 21, 30, 31, 36, 44, 50, 52, 55, 56, 59, 75, 80, 82, 85, 95, 97, 100-103, 105-107, 112, 119-121, 124-126, 144, 148

Black Hills Journal—107
Black Hills race track—72, 75
Black Kettle—27, 47
Black Moon—17, 45
Black Shawl—14, 22, 23
Blue Feather—122
Bluewater Creek fight—25, 27, 92
Board of Indian Commissioners—29, 99
Bodmer, Karl—114
Bordeaux, James—91
Bordeaux, Louis—23
Boston, Massachusetts—137
Bowen, Dr. Richard—147
Boy Scouts—139, 140
Bozeman, Montana—13
Bozeman Trail—13, 14, 58, 92, 94, 95
Brave Bear—25, 91
Brave Bull—36
Bridgeman, John—105
British Colombia—49, 66
Broken Bow—74
Brookings, South Dakota—129, 131, 132, 146, 147
Brotherton, Major—51
Brown, W. R.—79
Brules—11, 13, 20, 22, 23, 25-32, 35, 36, 39, 46, 64, 90, 92, 100, 101, 105, 106, 108, 109, 120, 122, 127
Brunot, Commissioner Felix R.—99
Buffalo Bill's Wild West Show—49, 51, 52
Bureau of Indian Affairs—139, 140
Buffalo Gap, South Dakota—97
Buffalo hunt—29, 114
Buffalo and railroad—42
Buffalo, skinning on prairie—30
Buffalo skull—160
Bugler (Max)—35
Bullhead, Lieutenant—53
Burden Brothers—124
Burleson, Bishop—123
Burning Breast, Lucy—127

Calhoun's company—63
Camp Chaffee—133
Camp Robinson—31, 32, 98
Camp Sheridan—30, 31
Canada—20, 21, 40, 49, 50, 66, 106, 124
Cannon Ball River—96
Carlisle, Pennsylvania—35
Carlisle University—35-37, 112, 114, 118, 120
Carrington, Colonel—94
Cedar Falls—78
Chandler, Secretary of the Interior Department—103
Charger—72, 82, 100
Charger, Harry—89
Charger, Martin—72-89
Charger, Philip E.—89
Charger, Samuel—72, 77, 82, 86, 89
Charging Dog—74, 77
Chase, Mrs. Mary Long—53
Chauncey Yellow Robe, see Yellow Robe, Chauncey

Cherokee, North Carolina—83
Cherry Creek—82
Cheyenne Agency—55, 82, 84, 85, 100
Cheyenne River—35, 40, 55, 82
Cheyenne River Agency—84
Cheyenne River Reservation—89
Cheyennes—17, 18, 20, 27, 28, 31, 44, 45, 46, 62, 64, 85, 90, 100
Cheyenne, Wyoming—13
Chicago—39, 49, 125
Chips—12, 13, 23
Chivington, Colonel J. M.—27
Choteau, P.—91
Churchill, Winston—133
City Park, Mobridge—87
Clark, General—22, 23
Clark, Lt. W. P.—106
Cleveland, President Grover—51
Cody, William F. (Buffalo Bill)—50, 51, 114, 115, 116
Colby, Frances Ryland—146
Colby, Irvin—146
Collier, John, Commissioner of Indian Affairs—130
Colorado volunteers—27
Company H—65
Company I—65
Commission of Indian Affairs—108
Commissioner of Indian Affairs—108
Community Action Agency—145
Conn, Mr. and Mrs. Herb—144
Conowicakte—112
Conquering Bear—90, 91, 98
Cook, Brigadier General John—78, 84, 36
Coolidge, President Calvin—120-124
Coolidge, John—120, 123
Coolidge, Mrs.—120-123
Cooper Institute—98
Corn Creek Community—23
Corps of Engineers—147
Cottage Grove, Oregon—127
Cottonwood—27
Council of 1864—27
Cox, Secretary of the Interior—97, 98
Crazy Horse—frontispiece, 11-24, 26, 31, 32, 45, 46, 49, 50, 55, 60, 66, 92, 94, 105, 106, 111, 112, 126, 147
Crazy Horse the Holy Man—12
Cronau, Dr. Rudolf—51
Crook, Brigadier General George—15-18, 21, 23, 31, 32, 59, 60, 97, 103, 104, 106
Crow Creek Reservation—112
Crow Dog—26, 33, 36-39, 47, 108
Crow Feather—74
Crowfoot—53
Crow King—17, 45
Crows—13, 43, 72, 74, 81, 90, 92, 147
Crowsheart—136
Crowsheart, Mrs. Helen—135
Cunka—26
Curly—11, 22
Custer Battlefield—65, 69
Custer Battlefield Museum—70
Custer Expedition of 1874—56

Custer, General George Armstrong—15, 18, 19, 20, 23, 30, 44-47, 49, 52, 59-64, 66-68, 82, 100, 103-105, 112, 119, 123
Custer Massacre—41
Custer, South Dakota—100, 144
Custer State Park—59
Custer's stone marker—70
Cutheads—95

Dakota Territory—21, 30, 32, 42, 52, 61, 64, 65, 75, 79, 80, 84, 96, 103
Dakotah—112
Dallas, Texas—133
Daniels, Agent J. W.—100
Dawes Act—83
Days of '76—120
Deadwood, South Dakota—38, 39, 107, 120
Deland, Dr. Charles E.—72
Department of the Interior—103
Dependable—72
Department of the Interior—103
Dependable—72
D Company, Seventh Cavalry—65
Delta, Colorado—145
Democratic Central Committee—145
Disabled American Veterans—140
Dominy, Floyd—143
DuBois, Rev. Charles G.—65
Dull Knife—21
Duly, Mr. and Mrs.—77-79
Dupree, Frederick—78
Durango, Colorado—146

Edgerly, Lieutenant W. Scott—65
Edmunds County, South Dakota—132
Eggen, C. Peter—144
Eighth Cavalry—55
Eisenhower, President Dwight D.—142
Elbowoods, North Dakota—134, 135
Elks Lodge—140
Eliza—84
El Paso, Texas—133
Enlisted men—62
Episcopal Hare School of Boys—129
Erwin, South Dakota—129, 143
Eskimos—144
Everett, Lillie—78, 79
Everett, Mr.—79
Everglades—132

Faculte de Medecine, Paris—125
Far West steamer—68, 105
Fechet, Major E. G.—52, 53
Female Deer—112
Fenn, Geraldine—147
Fetterman, Captain William Judd—13, 94
Fetterman Massacre—16
Fetterman Monument—16, 92
Field—84
Fighting cock of the Sioux—57
Finkbeiner, Professor Hans—125
Florida—132
Fool Soldiers—74-82, 87, 88
Fool Soldiers Monument—87
Forest City—82
Fort Abraham Lincoln—30, 59, 100
Fort Bennett—55
Fort Bennett Agency—81
Fort Berthold Indian Reservation—134-136, 138, 139
Fort Berthold, North Dakota—134
Fort Bliss—133
Fort Buford—51, 58, 66
Fort C. F. Smith—94, 95
Fort Custer—133
Fort Dodge, Iowa—79
Fort Ellis—59
Fort Fetterman—59, 97
Fort George—40
Fort Kearney—27
Fort LaFramboise—77, 78
Fort Laramie—15, 25, 27, 31, 40, 44, 57, 58, 74, 81, 88, 90, 94-96, 99

Fort Leavenworth—25-28
Fort Meade—64
Fort Phil Kearny—13, 14, 27, 94, 95
Fort Pierre—74, 75, 77, 78, 80, 81
Fort Randall—51, 77, 78, 80, 83
Fort Reno—95
Fort Rice—57, 58, 80
Fort Robinson—23, 32, 50, 66, 100, 105-107
Fort Shaw—59
Fort Smith—133
Fort Sully—42, 80, 100
Fort Yates—51-53, 65, 108
Four Bears—74, 77, 82, 85
Four Bears Monument—88
Four Horns—40
France—133
French Creek—100
Fulbright Award—125

Gall—17-19, 45, 49-51, 57-71, 105, 111, 126, 46
Gallagher, H. D.—110
Galpin, Charles—76-78
Garnett, Billy—23
Garrison Dam—88, 134-138
Garrison Reservoir—135
Garry Owen Historical marker—66, 70
Geiger—65
Genin, Reverend J. B. M.—46
Germany—125, 133
Gibbon, General John—15, 18, 45, 46, 59, 61, 64, 104
Gilbert, Luke—86
Gill, Bob—140
Gill, Paul—140
Goldwater, Barry—142
Grabber—22
Grand River—28, 51, 55, 78
Grant, President—31, 43, 44, 100, 103, 105
Grass Society—74
Grass, John—51, 67
Grattan, Lieutenant John—25, 90, 91
Grattan massacre—90
Gray Face—80
Gricer, Ernest—42
Gros Ventres—64, 90, 134, 135
Grouard, Frank—22, 23

Hangman's Hill—125
Hansen, Mrs. Julia—143
Hare, Bishop—83
Harney, General William S.—21, 25, 57, 74, 92
Harney Peak—100
Harrison, William Henry—143
Harvard University—137-139
Hayes, President—103
Hayt, Commissioner E. C.—35
Hazen, General—51
Heacock, Katherine—133
He Dog—13, 15, 20, 38
Henderson, Nevada—147
Her Good Road—72
Hidatsa—88, 135
Hieb, Dale—140
High Forehead—25, 90
High Hawk—47
His Horse Looking—12
Hitler—133
Holum, Ken—143
Honstad, Mrs. John—147
Hopkins—52
The Hornet—25, 74, 92
Horse bones—64
House Agriculture Committee—140
House Appropriations Committee—140
Howard, Agent—30
Howe, Oscar—81, 88
Hump—12, 13, 17, 45, 110
Hunkpapas—17, 18, 40, 42, 45, 46, 50, 57, 58, 59, 61, 64, 66-68, 74, 75, 95, 105, 122
Hunting His Lodge—40
Huron College—140

Idaho—76
Ilges, Major Guido—66
Indian Bureau—143
Indian camp—46
Indian Commissioners—106
Indian Council Fire Achievement Award—125, 139
Indian Cultural Parks—143
Indian lecturers at Custer Battlefield—70
Indian peace commissioners—94
Indian police—35, 36, 84, 104, 107, 108, 110
Indian Public Health Services—146
Indian Reorganization Act of 1932—130
Indian Ring—109
Interior Committee—140
Ipswich, South Dakota—140
Ireland girls—78

Jack Red Cloud—109
Jane Grey Bear—89
Japan—133
Jenney-Newton survey—75
Jenney, Walter P.—15, 30, 59, 100
Jewel Cave—144, 148
John Hay Whitney Fellowship—138
Johnson, Alice Janet—129, 132
Jumping Buffalo—26
Jumping Bull—40

Kennington, Captain—23
Keogh, Colonel—65
Keogh's company—63
Kicking Bear—52
Kill in Woods—112
Kills Game and Comes Back—74, 77, 78, 80
Kingsbury, George W.—46, 67, 101
Knights Templar—125
Korn, Gustave—64
Kraus, Ethel—127
Krull, J. E.—144

Lacota oyate—112
LaCroix, Art—145
Lake Shetak—78
Lakotas—16
LaPlant, Louis—72, 78, 82
LaPlant, South Dakota—89
Larrabee, Joe—22
Larrabee, Nellie—21, 22, 24
Leading Eagle—122, 123
Leavenworth, Kansas—28, 133
Leavenworth Times, Kansas—65
Lee, Lieutenant Jesse M.—31, 35
Legislative Subcommittee—140
Lewis and Clark—72, 147
Lewis and Clark—72, 147
Lewis, Meriwether—72
Lewis, Reuben—72
Littauer School of Public Administration—137
Little Bell—48
Little Bend—82
Little Big Horn—17, 18, 45, 46, 59-62, 66, 69, 123
Little Big Man—23
Little Hawk—15, 72
Little Owl—136
Little Pete—135, 136
Little Scout (Pollock)—35
Little Spotted Tail—39
Little Thunder—27, 74
Little Wolf—23, 95
Little Wound—99, 105, 111
London—51
Lone Bear—23
Lone Feather—127, 133
Long Chin—25
Los Angeles, California—147
Low Dog—17, 45
Lower Platte—27

Mad Bear—77
Mahkpia-luta—90

Man Afraid, see Man Afraid of His Horses
Man Afraid of His Horses—90, 92, 100, 102, 105
Mancos Canyon Ute Mountain Ute Reservation—146
Mandans—72, 76, 88, 134-136
Marias River—43
Masonic Lodge—118, 125, 140
Mass Monument at Custer Battlefield—67
Matotopa—82
Maynadier, Colonel—27
Maynard, Clair F.—125, 126
McDougall, Captain—61
McGillycuddy, Dr. Valentine T.—23, 43, 99, 102-110
McGillycuddy, Mrs.—108
McGovern, George—143
McLaughlin, South Dakota—144
Meckling—65
Medicine Bear's wife—38
Medicine Creek—80
Merritt, Colonel—20
Messiah Craze—51, 52, 68, 83, 111, 110, 115
Michigan—133
Miles, General Nelson A.—19, 20, 21, 52, 116
Military men—61
Military Police—133
Minneconjous—17, 25, 45, 46, 53, 55, 64, 82, 90, 95, 100, 105, 115
Minnesota—75, 76, 78, 131
Mission, South Dakota—38, 141
Mississippi River—110
Missouri River—11, 15, 22, 26, 28, 29, 32, 35, 40, 42, 51, 55, 57, 74, 76, 80, 82, 96, 100, 103, 106, 134, 136, 137, 138, 143, 147, 160
Mobridge, South Dakota—55, 81, 86, 88
Montana—31, 43, 66, 92, 112, 131
Mormon cow—25, 90
Mountain View Cemetery—125
Mount Holyoke College—125
Mount Rushmore—11, 125
Mundt, Karl—143
Mydland, General Gordon—143

National Easter Seal Society—140
National Geographic Society—131
National Parks Service—142-144, 146
Nebraska—29, 36, 112, 130
Nevada—52
Newell, Agent Cicero—35, 36
New York—79, 113, 124, 125
New York Herald—99
New York Standard—98
New York Times—98
Nez Perces—22
Nichols, Mrs. Eva J.—145
Nielsen, Nell—125
Niobrara Convocation of the Protestant Episcopal Church—123
Nixon, President Richard M.—145
Norbeck, Peter—89
North Dakota—44, 59, 88, 100, 110, 112, 130, 135-138
North Dakota Historical Collections—46
Northern Pacific Railway—15, 40, 42, 43, 59, 100
North Platte, Nebraska—28, 29, 90
Northwestern University—125
No Water—13, 13, 22, 23

Oahe Dam—86
Oahe Irrigation Project Committee—143
Officers of the western army—63
Oglalas—11, 12, 14, 15, 17, 18, 20-24, 32, 45, 46, 49, 50, 59, 64, 66, 90, 92, 95-102, 105, 106, 108, 110, 111, 133, 143
Oglala town—129
Ohio—143
Oklahoma—125
Old Settlers' Association of Walworth County—86
Omaha, Nebraska—25, 105, 144
One Feather—72

One Ghost—80
One Rib—77
One That Had Four Robes, The—40
Oregon Trail—92
Outstanding American Indian Award—139

Parker, Indian Commissioner—97
Parmelee, South Dakota—127, 136
Pattee, Colonel John—75, 78, 79, 83
Pawnees—25, 27
Pearl Harbor—133
Pennington County Democratic Advisory Committee—145
Pennsylvania—89
Permanent Camp—100
Philadelphia—89
Pierre Indian School—147
Pierre, South Dakota—130, 131, 160
Pine Ridge—20, 36, 50, 105-108, 132
Pine Ridge Agency—24, 50, 98, 99, 101, 103, 104, 106, 110, 114, 115, 130
Pine Ridge Reservation—23, 110, 111, 112, 123, 129, 131, 133, 139
Pizi—57
Platte River—25, 27, 29, 40, 90
Point of Rocks—97
Pollock, W. J.—35
Ponca Creek—78
Poplar River Agency—66
Porcupine—52
Pourier, Big Bat—17, 22
Pratt, Captain R. H.—35, 114
Pretty Bear—77
Price, S. Goodale—65
Primeau, Charles—77, 78
Promise, John—83
Powder River—13-17, 27, 28, 32, 43, 49, 59, 92, 96, 104, 106

Quick Bear—36

Rain in the Face—17, 45
Rapid City Journal—65, 143
Rapid City Public Health Service Indian Hospital—146
Rapid City, South Dakota—39, 72, 107, 112, 114, 116-119, 124-126, 133, 144, 145
Raw Hide Buttes—99
Red Cloud—13-15, 20, 22, 23, 26, 28-32, 36, 58, 90-112, 121, 126
Red Cloud Agency—20, 21, 22, 31, 32, 36, 42, 50, 66, 82, 100, 105, 106, 139
Red Cloud Reservation—43
Red Cloud's wife—93
Red Cloud War—94
Red Dog—77, 96, 101, 105
Red God of Nevada, The—52
Red Leaf—25
Red River—88
Red River Cart—81, 88
Red Road—35
Red Shirt—105
Rees, see Aricara
Reifel, Albert—127, 130, 147
Reifel, Alex—127, 130, 147
Reifel, Alice—130-134, 136, 137, 141-143, 146
Reifel, Ben—127-148
Reifel, George—127, 130, 147
Reifel, John—127, 130, 147
Reifel, Loyce—131-134, 136, 137
Reifel, Lucy—127, 130, 136
Reifel, William—127, 129, 130
Related Agencies Committee—140
Reno Creek—63
Reno, Major Marcus A.—18, 19, 46, 49, 57, 60-70
Reno Monument—67
Republican Fork—27, 29
Republican Party—140, 142-144
Republican River—90
Reynolds, Colonel—15
R. H. Donnelly Advertising—125
Richard, John—98
Ring Thunder—38

Risley, Agent—29
Riverside Park—86-88
Robinson, Doane—72, 80
Rockefeller Institute Hospital—124
Rocky Mountains—52
Roosevelt, Franklin—133
Rosa Red Weasel—89
Rosebud Agency—35, 36, 38, 39
Rosebud Agency Government Day School—127
Rosebud Boarding School—147
Rosebud Creek—17, 18, 35, 36, 45, 50, 60, 61, 106
Rosebud Reservation—39, 112, 125, 127, 129, 141
Roseth, Clayton—140
Rotary—140
ROTC—129, 131
Running Horse (High Standing Soldier)—35

Sacred Stand—41
Sacred Standshoty—41
Sandoz, Mari—11, 18, 20, 23, 24
Sans Arc—17, 45, 46, 72, 74, 75, 80-83, 95, 105
Santees—29, 42, 46, 75-78, 80, 81, 82, 95, 105
Saone—26
Schurz, Secretary of the Interior Carl—35, 37, 107, 108
Secondary South Dakota School of Agriculture—129
Seventh Cavalry—18, 20, 46, 52, 55, 60-62, 65, 68, 82, 104, 115, 66
Seventeenth Infantry—60
Seymour, A. E.—124
Sheridan, Lt. Gen. Philip H.—15, 18, 23, 59, 104
Sheridan, Wyoming—139
Shetak captives—72, 77-78
Shirt Wearers—13, 14, 22, 27, 92, 106
Short Bull—20, 52
Shorty—127
Shrine of Democracy—125
Shunk, Harold—145
Sibley, General—20
Silent Enemy, The—113, 123, 124
Sinte Galeska—25, 26
Sintegaleska Chika—39
Sioux City, Iowa—78, 79, 100
Sioux grave—79
Sioux Indian village—frontispiece
Sioux Sanatorium Day School—125
Sioux squaws—45
Sisphi—46
Sisseton, South Dakota—141, 144
Sisseton Reservation—112
Sissetons—42
Sitting Bull, Hunkpapa—15, 17-21, 31, 40-56, 57, 59-62, 66-68, 83, 104-106, 108, 110-112, 115, 121, 122, 126
Sitting Bull, Oglala—15, 42
Sixth Infantry—60
Slim Buttes—80
Slow—41
Smith, Commissioner of Indian Affairs E. P.
Society of American Indians—116
Sophie Left Handed Bear—89
South America—136
South Dakota—11, 15, 26, 35, 44, 52, 53, 55, 72, 80, 89, 94, 110, 112, 114, 116, 122, 125, 127, 128, 130, 131, 136, 139, 140, 142, 143, 146
South Dakota Historical Society—86
South Dakota School of Mines—119
South Dakota State College—129, 131, 147
Spotted Eagle—17, 45
Spotted Tail—11, 15, 20, 21, 25-39, 94, 96-98, 100, 101, 103, 105, 106, 108, 109, 111, 112, 121, 122, 126
Spotted Tail Agency—23, 29, 30, 31, 38, 50, 82, 100, 106
Spotted Tail Monument—125
Spotted Tail's Friendly Band—28
Spotted Tail's sons—35, 36, 37
Spotted Tail's wife—29
Standing Bear, Henry—24, 36, 120, 122

Standing Rock Agency—44, 51, 53, 66, 67
Standing Rock Reservation—67, 70, 83, 110
Stanley, General D. S.—42
Stays at Home (William)—35
Stephenson, Adelaide—136
Stevens, Captain Albert W.—131
St. Louis—72
Strange Man—12, 15, 24
Stratosphere flights—131
Strikes Fire—77
Stuart, Gen.—23
Sturgis—72
Sumner, Colonel E. V.—55
Sun Dance—11, 25, 32, 35
Swan—82
Swan, Carroll—145
Swift Bear—23, 27, 29
Swift Bird—74, 77
Sword, George—13, 20, 21, 92, 104, 106, 107, 108, 110

Tackett, Charles—35
Tahcawin—112
Talks With Bear (Oliver)—35
Tall Mandan—76
Tangle Hair—26
Tasinagi—112
TaTanKa YoTanKa—41, 43
Terry, Brigadier General Alfred H.—15, 18, 19, 45, 46, 49, 59, 61, 62, 64, 104
Tetons—46, 47, 64
They Are Afraid of Her—14
Thunder Hawk—36
Thunderhead Mountain—11, 24
Todd, Dave—144
Tongue River—18, 21, 45
Touch the Clouds—23
Treaty of 1851—74, 90-92
Treaty of 1856—74
Treaty of 1862—27
Treaty of 1866—27, 58, 94
Treaty of 1868—15, 28, 40, 44, 47, 58, 59, 81, 94, 95, 98
Treaty of 1874—100
Treaty of 1876 (Black Hills)—20, 31, 66, 77, 82, 88, 96, 105
Treaty of 1889—83
Tribal Council—135, 137
Turkey Head—72, 76
Two Kettles—46, 76, 77, 82, 88, 95, 105
Two Moon—17, 45
Two Strike—26, 27, 33, 38, 39, 47, 111

Ulke, H.—34
Uncpapas, see Hunkpapas
Union Pacific Railroad—27
United States—133
United States Cavalry Troop I—64
United States Congress—127, 140, 141
United States Department of Agriculture—129, 132
United States Indian School—112, 114, 118-120
University of South Dakota—88, 147
University of South Dakota Development Committee—140
Upper Midwest Regional Educational Laboratory—140
Upper White River—29
Ute Mountain Ute Tribe—146

Vassar—125
Vermillion, South Dakota—88, 147
Veterans Administration Clinic—147
Veterans of Foreign Wars—140
Vik, Mrs. Della B.—124, 125
Virginia—135
Voit—65

Wa-ana-tan—72, 82
Wagon Box Fight—13, 94
Wahzazhe—90
Walking Hail—74, 84
Walks With The Pipe—26
Walter Reed Hospital—143
Wamblee, South Dakota—120
Wamblee-Tokaha—122, 123
Washington, D. C.—27-30, 32, 33, 35, 42, 51, 68, 81, 83-85, 92, 95-97, 99-101, 105, 106, 108-111, 137, 139, 140, 142-145, 147
Was Seen By The Nation—40
Wasumaniwin (Eliza)—84
Watertown, South Dakota—131, 144
Waukazoo, Mrs. Muriel—145
Wavoka—52, 110
WCAT—119
Weir, Captain—65
Welsh, William—29
West Beaver Creek—30, 32
Wheat Flower—27
Wheeler Howard Act—131
Whetstone Agency—29, 97
Whetstone Creek—28
Whispering Smith—128, 137
White Bull—17, 45

White Cow Bull—133
White Horse, Lee—125
White Horse, Mrs. Lee—39
White Lodge—76
White Rain Mountains—64
White River—23, 26, 28-30, 100
Whiteside, Major—55
White Thunder—39
Wilde, Mr. and Mrs.—135
Wilhelm, Gene—143
Willow Creek—40
Wilson, Jack—52
Windolph, Charles—65
Wirwan, Mike—143
Wiyaka Wanjila—127, 133
Woman's Dress—13, 20-23
Works Progress Administration—129, 130
World War II—134
Worm—13, 23
Wounded Knee—54, 55, 68, 83, 95, 111, 114-116, 118, 123, 124
Wowacinye—72
Wright, Mrs. Julia—77, 78, 84
Wright, Mr.—79
Wyoming—17, 59, 66, 92, 94, 112, 143
Wyoming mountains—64

Yankton Agency—79, 84
Yankton Agency Mission School—83
Yanktonnais—42, 75, 95, 105
Yankton steamboat landing—84
Yellow Buckskin Girl—27, 31
Yellow Hair—49, 112
Yellow Hand—20
Yellow Medicine Indian Agency—75
Yellow Robe—112
Yellow Robe, Chauncey—112-126
Yellow Robe, Chauncey, Jr.—118, 126
Yellow Robe, Chauncina—39, 114, 117, 118, 125
Yellow Robe, Evenlyn—118, 125
Yellow Robe, Mrs.—117, 118
Yellow Robe, Rosebud—114, 117, 118, 121-125
Yellowstone River—15, 18, 22, 45, 59, 61, 76
Young Man Afraid, see Young Man Afraid of His Horses
Young Man Afraid of His Horses—13-15, 20, 26, 50, 90, 92, 101, 102, 106, 107, 108, 110, 111

Ziolkowski, Korczak—11, 24, 55
Zion National Park—142

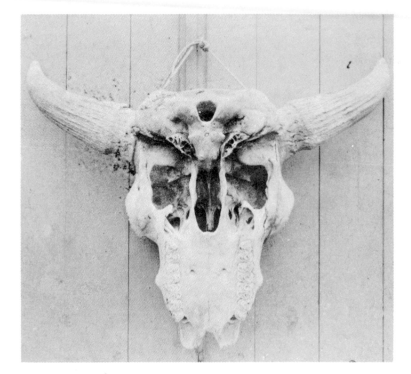

Buffalo skull found at Pierre, South Dakota, on the left bank of the Missouri River in November 1905. The Indian buffalo economy today is as dead as this buffalo skull, Reifel emphasizes, and the Indian has moved into the present and toward the future. (Photo by courtesy of Ralph H. Finley)